Opting Out of War

Opting Out of War

Strategies to Prevent Violent Conflict

Mary B. Anderson and
Marshall Wallace

Viva Books
New Delhi | Mumbai | Chennai | Kolkata | Bengaluru | Hyderabad | Kochi | Guwahati

First Indian Edition 2013

VIVA BOOKS PRIVATE LIMITED

- 4737/23 Ansari Road, Daryaganj, New Delhi 110 002
  E-mail: vivadelhi@vivagroupindia.net, Tel. 42242200
- 76, Service Industries, Shirvane, Sector 1, Nerul, Navi Mumbai 400 706
  E-mail: vivamumbai@vivagroupindia.net, Tel. 27721273, 27721274
- Jamals Fazal Chambers, 26 Greams Road, Chennai 600 006
  E-mail: vivachennai@vivagroupindia.net, Tel. 28290304, 28294241
- B-103, Jindal Towers, 21/1A/3 Darga Road, Kolkata 700 017
  E-mail: vivakolkata@vivagroupindia.net, Tel. 22836381, 22816713
- 7, Sovereign Park Apartments, 56-58, K. R. Road, Basavanagudi, Bengaluru 560 004
  E-mail: vivabangalore@vivagroupindia.net, Tel. 26607409, 26607410
- 101-102 Mughal Marc Apartments, 3-4-637 to 641, Narayanguda, Hyderabad 500 029
  E-mail: vivahyderabad@vivagroupindia.net, Tel. 27564481, 27564482
- Beevi Towers, First Floor, SRM Road, Kaloor, Kochi 682 018, Kerala
  E-mail: vivakochi@vivagroupindia.net, Tel: 0484-2403055, 2403056
- 232, GNB Road, Beside UCO Bank, Silpukhuri, Guwahati 781 003
  E-mail: vivaguwahati@vivagroupindia.net, Tel: 0361-2666386

www.vivagroupindia.com

Published by arrangement with

Lynne Rienner Publishers, Inc.
1800 30th Street, Suite 314
Boulder, Colorado 80301
USA

ISBN : 978-81-309-2372-7

Published by Vinod Vasishtha for Viva Books Private Limited, 4737/23, Ansari Road, Daryaganj, New Delhi-110 002. Printed and bound by Saurabh Printers, New Delhi.

Contents

Part 3 Conclusion

Preface

Writing this book has been both heartening and challenging. We have been moved by the experiences of the thirteen nonwar communities explored in this book. These communities developed imaginative and innovative strategies that enabled them to stay out of the wars surrounding them. Their bravery and cleverness are impressive and inspiring. Getting to know them and their experiences through the case studies we have gathered here has been a delight, full of twists and turns that we had not foreseen or imagined possible. People are capable of analyzing their own circumstances—even overwhelming circumstances—and coming up with ideas and options for living through adversity that strengthen rather than weaken their values and community cohesion.

We have been challenged by these case studies as well. The nature of the experiences of the nonwar communities posed problems. People told their stories in localized ways relating to the particularities of their own wars, their own warriors, their own communities, and their own decisions. They did not try to extrapolate from their experiences to provide ideas to others. Their claims were immediate and pragmatic, not universal and generalizable.

Therefore, as we learned of each case and its specialness, it became our job to extrapolate lessons that could be of use to others. That there were patterns and commonalities across the cases became clear very early on. The challenge was how to identify these patterns and commonalities without neglecting the nuance and depth of each particular story.

This would have been impossible without the involvement of many people. First, of course, are the communities themselves. Their willingness to tell their stories and share their experiences was kind and generous. We are indeed indebted to them, both for the fact that they invented strategies for exempting themselves from war and for their readiness to spend time with case writers to explain why and how they did this.

Second are the case-writing teams who visited the communities and chronicled their stories. The teams showed sensitivity and insight as they found their way into the histories and experiences of the communities. They needed to listen and learn, setting aside many preconceptions about conflict prevention, and they did so admirably. In addition, many of the writers joined consultations with writers of other cases and, by reflecting on what they had heard in each place, helped identify and explore the common themes of the experiences of these communities. Their thoughts, as much as our own, have shaped the learning reported in the chapters that follow. The case writers include for Afghanistan, Mohammad Suleman and Sue Williams; for Bosnia-Herzegovina, Vasiliki Neofotistos and Marshall Wallace; for Burkina Faso, Mark Canavera; for Colombia, Luis Enrique Eguren and Liam Mahony; for Fiji, Kristin Doughty, Satendra Prasad, and Darryn Snell; for India, Urvashi Butalia; for Kosovo, David Reyes; for Mozambique, Tarah Farman with Ezequiel Marcos and Egidio Vaz; for Nigeria, Austin Onuoha and Lynda Lolo; for the Philippines (Mindanao), Pushpa Iyer; for Rwanda, Kristen Doughty and David Moussa Ntambara; for Sierra Leone, Lawrence G. Dixon and Samuel Mokuwa; and for Sri Lanka, Greg Hansen. Our thanks to them is boundless!

Third, and also essential to the success of this project, are the donors who generously and faithfully provided the funding. They include the German Church Development Service (Evangelischer Entwicklungsdienst [EED]), the Ministry of Foreign Affairs of Denmark, the Netherlands Ministry of Foreign Affairs (Ministerie van Buitenlandse Zaken [BuZa]), the Norwegian Ministry of Foreign Affairs, the Swedish International Development Cooperation Agency (SIDA), and the US Agency for International Development (USAID). We thank them for their readiness to enable our search for learning without the certainty that lessons would be forthcoming. This kind of donorship, we believe, is an essential aspect of the continuing learning that is important to improving the effectiveness of international collaboration.

In some countries, agencies and nongovernmental organizations, both international and local, opened doors for case writers and provided hospitality. These are too numerous to list here, as the generosity of our colleagues and their interest in this project exceeded our expectations. Wherever the case writers asked for an interview or advice or assistance, the response was immediate and generous. We thank these agencies and organizations for their colleagueship, their kindness, and their unflagging energy.

Finally, our fellow staff members at CDA Collaborative Learning Projects provided support, encouragement, ideas, and critiques. By reading and commenting on early drafts of our case studies, sitting with us in discussions of our findings, listening to and critiquing our ponderings, and supporting the mechanical production of our manuscript, they contributed greatly. Special thanks go to Candice Montalvo, who managed the formatting of the entire manuscript; Nicole Goddard, for engaging our ideas and lessons learned; and Dayna Brown, Steve Darvill, Ana Paula do Nascimento, and Peter Woodrow, for their careful reading and useful comments on early drafts.

Nonetheless, of course, despite the involvement of the thousands of people who made this book and the fruition of its ideas possible, we as the authors bear responsibility for any errors of analysis or misinterpretations of the material presented here.

One more pleasure that must be named is the response of many of the nonwar communities to their interactions with the case writers. In virtually every case, people in these communities thanked the case writers for coming to investigate their stories. Some said that other international actors had come to see them to learn why they were struggling economically or politically, but never to ask them about their successes. Others commented that they themselves had not thought of their actions as interesting and worthy of analysis until the case writers asked them to reflect. Through collecting their memories and reflecting upon them, they were surprised to learn more from their own experience than they had before the case writers arrived.

The case writers who visited Jaghori in Afghanistan captured this in their report, in the words of one community member who reflected: "Until recently, we knew war, we knew fighting, we knew how to use guns to get what we wanted. After defeating the Taliban, we gave up our guns willingly. Now we understand the benefits of peace, the disadvantages of war. This kind of discussion has reminded us of the good things we have, the solidarity, our own good leadership. We must make the same sacrifice we made for the jihad, but now for peace."

—Mary B. Anderson and
Marshall Wallace

Opting Out of War

1

Preventing Violent Conflict

Why is the prevention of violent conflict so difficult? International actors agree that prevention is preferable to and less expensive than humanitarian assistance or postconflict reconstruction. Donor countries have adopted broad policies and initiated funding and programming mechanisms to support prevention. Attention is given to early warning systems designed to alert diplomats and aid-providers to impending conflicts so that they can act in timely, preventive ways. Still, conflicts occur.

This is particularly puzzling because war is, oddly, an unnatural institution. It requires organization, money, charisma, and sacrifice. In the twenty-first century, active warfare is not now, if it ever were, the normal state of affairs. Statistically, more countries do not engage in war than do, and where war occurs, more people do not actively participate than do. War is in this sense a fragile undertaking; most people, including many in the highest echelons of military defense forces, want and work to avoid it.

Nonetheless, war continues to be common, enduring, and persistent. There are few locations and few individuals who are not somehow affected by it. Defense budgets are sizable and supported by the taxes citizens pay. The news heard and read around the globe carries regular stories of war-related injuries, destruction, and death. There seems to be a threat of war somewhere in the world at all times. It appears that people and societies slip into warfare almost without thought if they feel threatened by others. Although people want to avoid war, most accept that it is natural and necessary to fight for certain values. Once war begins, ending it requires intense and long-term efforts of many actors.

If most people want to avoid war and its costs are so high, why is it also common? If war requires an unnatural effort, why does preventing violent conflict remain elusive? Perhaps part of the reason can be found in the approaches taken by most international conflict prevention efforts. Largely, these focus in four areas.[1] Some emphasize early warning as essential for initiating preventive activity. Some focus on dispute resolution tools such as mediation, trust-building processes, or diplomacy. Some take an educational or training approach, with the expectation that alternative conflict resolution skills and techniques or new attitudes can enable leaders and communities to resolve differences without resorting to violence. Finally, some focus on changing structures that divide people and building the institutions of statehood (good governance, strong judiciaries, well-trained and disciplined police, secure economies), with the expectation that where such institutions exist, conflict is less likely to occur compared to places where they are missing or weak. Even as these approaches differ, they often involve bringing something new to conflict-prone environments to enable people in these places to avert violence.[2]

Largely missing, however, from many (possibly most) international efforts to prevent conflict, is acknowledgment that systems and skills to prevent overt violence between groups already exist in every society.[3] In fact, violence is regularly prevented even in conflict-prone areas. Local people have structures and connections that they use to maintain peace day by day in their own space. Communities who want to avoid violence often find ways to do so—at least for a time.

If war breaks out and widespread violence occurs, this of course indicates that existing prevention systems were not strong enough. Worse, war itself causes many preexisting connections to fail. As a result, most observers—both insiders and outsiders—conclude that new systems need to be imagined and created to enable a warring society to become peaceful.

This conclusion is undoubtedly true, but it may be less true than we imagine. A closer examination of areas of conflict reveals that, in the midst of war, some communities—sometimes quite sizable and significant—develop strategies by which to exempt themselves from participation in surrounding violence. In this sense, some communities, despite prevailing pressures and often without outside help, successfully prevent conflict.[4]

The Value of Community-Based Conflict Prevention: Relevant Lessons for Larger Efforts?

In this book we approach the issue of conflict prevention from the perspective of such communities that in their own settings succeeded in preventing violence. The book tells the stories of thirteen communities of people—living in circumstances where all the forces and incentives that surrounded them seemingly should have pushed them into conflict—who somehow, as a group, decided not to fight and instead developed strategies for exempting themselves from war. In eleven of the stories the communities literally maintained a nonwar stance in the midst of surrounding civil war.[5] In the other two, an entire nation, where all the early warning indicators of impending conflict were high, managed repeatedly to step back from the brink. All these communities managed to exempt themselves from participation in the wars that others around them willingly and unwillingly were drawn into.

The locations of these thirteen communities are not unique. Around the world wherever conflict occurs, we have heard stories of similar groups. These thirteen provide examples of strategies and processes for avoiding participation in conflict that very likely exist more often and in more warring areas than we usually recognize.

The stories are interesting and impressive in and of themselves. But beyond that, by describing, comparing, and analyzing these thirteen examples, we intend to add to and broaden the discussion of how conflict prevention can work in other locations. How have these communities succeeded in opting out of war? Do their strategies hold any relevant lessons for broader peacemaking efforts undertaken by international actors? These are the questions that we explore.

Where This Evidence Comes From

Some years ago, as they visited numerous warring societies to work with aid-providers, two international humanitarian workers began to hear of communities in conflict areas that had somehow managed to avoid participation in war.[6] These communities were described not as pacifists or antiwar activists but as normal cities, villages, or regions that had managed to not take part in war and had survived without suffering the extensive damage experienced by most surrounding communities. Clearly, this was intriguing.

Prompted by these stories, CDA Collaborative Learning Projects (CDA)[7] initiated a project called Steps Toward Conflict Prevention (STEPS). From 2002 to 2006, CDA organized a process, generously supported by several donor countries (named in the preface to this book), through which observers visited the nonwar communities, talked with and heard from many people about what had happened, how, and why, and wrote these stories into case studies. In most cases, a two-person team, one a local person with broad access across the community and one an international visitor who had some background in conflict prevention, made the visit together. The stories vary in length and depth, partly reflecting the amount of time the teams were able to spend with the communities. However, each provides perspectives and insights that, cumulatively across contexts, add up to a surprising body of evidence.

The Experience

These thirteen case studies of nonwar communities will be quoted and referenced extensively. Five of them are more fully covered in Part 2 of this book in order to illustrate, in some detail, the ways in which the communities made collective choices and developed common strategies for staying out of conflict. These are:

- Afghanistan, where the Jaghori district in Ghazni province "surrendered" to the Taliban rather than fight against it, managing not only to not succumb to the Taliban's agenda but also to maintain its own way of life and values.
- Bosnia, where Tuzla managed to maintain its multiethnicity despite the agenda promoted by political and military leaders intent on establishing ethnically exclusive states in the former Yugoslavia.
- Colombia, where three indigenous communities developed strategies to assert themselves as "peace villages" and avoided conscription and involvement in the conflict between government, paramilitary, and rebel armed groups.

- Mozambique, where a region of Gaza province, under the protection of the ancestral spirit of Mungoi (a deceased former chief), was able to maintain roads, schools, and agricultural production even as surrounding areas were looted and destroyed.
- Rwanda, where the Muslim community, comprising both Hutus and Tutsis, did not participate in the genocide that engulfed the country in 1994 and instead managed to rescue many who would have been victims.

Two of these five case studies come from Africa, and one each comes from Europe, Asia, and Latin America. The conflicts they report on range from a hundred days (Rwanda) to four decades (Colombia) in length. They include diverse geographical areas, ranging from villages (Colombia) to districts (Mozambique and Afghanistan) to a dispersed population (Rwanda) to a sizable industrial city (Bosnia). The driving forces behind their avoidance of war range from religious belief (Rwanda), to an injunction from an ancestral spirit (Mozambique), to the political leadership of an elected mayor (Tuzla), to encouragement from outside human rights and church groups (Colombia), to the savvy calculations of a traditional council (Afghanistan). These five cases have been chosen for fuller inclusion in Part 2 because they represent the variety and complexity of the experiences of all thirteen of the nonwar communities and, at the same time, illustrate the patterns and common approaches discussed in Part 1.

The other eight cases provide similar evidence of the differences and commonalities of these nonwar communities,[8] as the following brief overviews make apparent.

Fiji and Burkina Faso

These two countries (as compared to the preceding examples, which represent subgroups within a country) have repeatedly come to the brink of war but, to date, have avoided full-scale fighting. In the case of Fiji, there were several coups d'état and instances of significant intergroup violence. However, the Fiji experience also contained a strong narrative about consistent "connectors" that kept the Indo-Fijians and the indigenous Fijians interlinked. In Burkina Faso, also a country that has experienced a coup d'état, a fascinating range of national strategies was developed to encourage a shared identity and commitment to living without intergroup violence. The experiences of these two countries provide a counterbalance for the smaller-scale cases in that they challenge any analysis that oversimplifies the decision to step away from war. They make abundantly clear that the ability to stay out of war is not an issue of scale; rather it is, indeed as the other cases also show, the result of conscious, collective decisions and choices.

India

In 1992, in India's northeastern state of Manipur, violent clashes broke out between two tribal groups, the Nagas and the Kukis. The clashes left an estimated 1,000 people dead and as many as 130,000 displaced and, as a result, ethnically mixed villages, once common in Manipur, almost ceased to exist. Even as the violence flared, "some places managed to retain a modicum of peace and harmony." They adopted varying strategies and approaches that worked to prevent armed groups from conquering or coercing them into joining the conflict.

Kosovo

The motivations and actions of groups within four communities in Kosovo provide insights into their collective opting out of participation in the 1999 conflict that are, in this case, both revealing and puzzling. One community, for example, was known to have aligned itself, and provided support to, one side of the conflict. Still, according to their own accounts, people in these villages did not engage in the war and, according to the accounts of others, found effective ways of avoiding the destruction that came to many surrounding areas that were drawn into the war. These villagers defined themselves as people who did not participate in the ethnic divisions of the war.

Nigeria

The Niger Delta region is known worldwide for the violence of the people's reactions toward international oil companies that operate there and toward their national government. The Ukwa area, where about 100,000 people live in twenty-three villages, is described as home to people who "in the midst of this madness . . . decided to keep the peace." Throughout the area, many people described a combination of factors that shaped their collective community choices to refuse to fight either oil companies or government. They claimed their stance was "only natural" and based in their history and training, though they acknowledged that their choices differed strikingly from those of neighboring communities and regions.

Philippines

Armed struggle in Mindanao has sometimes been attributed to tensions between Christians and Muslims or between tribal groupings (sometimes overlapping with religious affiliation); in other analyses, it has been traced to postcolonial land allocation and other economic disparities. In this context, numerous communities have been involved in the war but some, having previously engaged in or experienced violence, rejected further involvement and established themselves as zones or areas of peace. Often prompted or supported by Philippine and international nongovernmental organizations, they established intercommunal forums for discussion and planning and, in many instances, engaged commanders of opposing armed groups to join them in their ceremonies to exempt themselves from the war. As in Colombia, these Mindanao communities linked economic progress with avoidance of future violence and emphasized development as the basis of their strategies for nonengagement.

Sierra Leone

The village of Lawana, in the Moyamba district of Sierra Leone, was founded by a powerful warrior who "only wanted to protect and defend his village rather than attack and suppress others." This village and its chief developed strategies to avoid invasion or attack, and even to prevent the recruitment of its young men into the fighting forces, throughout the civil war between the Sierra Leone Army (SLA) and the Revolutionary United Front (RUF) that lasted from 1991 until 2002. Citing its history as one that prevented it from ever being invaded, these villagers welcomed anyone who sought refuge, hosting as many as 500 internally displaced persons (IDPs) in their homes and sharing their farmland so these strangers could support themselves. But even as they welcomed all strangers and gave them support, the Lawana villagers maintained secret codes for communication and a variety of strategies for escape, hiding, and engaging with armed groups—all in order to avoid being forced to take part in a conflict that engulfed most other surrounding villages.

Sri Lanka

Madhu, a 400-year-old shrine carved out of the dense forest in northern Sri Lanka, has attracted hundreds of thousands of pilgrims from all parts of Sri Lanka and from all faiths and ethnic groups over many years. During the long-lasting war between the government of Sri Lanka and the Tamil Tigers, this place became recognized as a sanctuary and safe space for all who wanted to escape the destruction and violence of the conflict. Working with the United Nations High Commissioner for Refugees (UNHCR), whose mission was to provide safe locations for displaced people inside Sri Lanka in order to curtail vast refugee movements to India, the bishop of Madhu negotiated with both the government and the Tamil leadership to guarantee their respect for the neutrality of the sanctuary and its security from armed groups.

* * *

These brief overviews and the five fuller cases in Part 2 do more than illustrate complexity, variety, and commonalities. They also show differences in outcomes. None of the stories is simple and straightforward. Some communities were more and some were less successful in providing security for their members. Some came closer to capitulation with armed groups while others maintained stronger separation. Solidarity varied and in some cases wavered. All these communities succeeded sometimes and failed at other times. The choices they made were deeply local, based on their best analysis of their circumstances at the time.

It is important to note here that the strategies of nine of the thirteen communities share a set of common elements that constitute the core of the chapters in Part 1. Another four of the communities shared some of these common features but were weak in others. As the stories unfold, these variations will become clear.

Nonetheless, the overarching lesson of these stories is one of existing capacities. In areas where war was being waged, these communities had the capacities to opt out of the conflict and to develop strategies by which they survived without joining sides. Taken together, their stories provide useful insights into the capacities needed to prevent conflict. They show that such capacities exist—even in warring areas—far more often than is usually recognized or acknowledged.

How This Book Is Organized

The evidence from all the cases is presented in Part 1 under the topics that emerged as the most important in determining how successful the communities were in preventing involvement in conflict. Chapter 2 looks at three steps each community took to establish itself as exempt from engaging in the conflict it faced. Chapter 3 discusses the importance of governance and of normalcy for maintaining community cohesion over the long term. Setting itself apart from war was not, as the evidence shows, a onetime decision by a community, but rather required daily, constant reinvigoration. Chapter 4 describes the systems and processes of nonwar governance by considering the roles of leadership and of communication. It discusses how leadership worked both to lead and to reflect popular will, ensuring that the decisions and choices made included everyone, reflected a broad consensus, and reinforced community cohesion. Chapter 5 then describes how these nonwar communities interacted with armed groups, reaching out to them but refusing to submit to them. Chapter 6 reviews the roles of international actors in each of the locations, examining how these roles both harmed and helped the processes of conflict prevention. Chapter 7 concludes Part 1 with a summary and consolidation of these experiences that shows how the approaches of these communities can be combined into a complete nonwar strategy.

Part 2, as mentioned, provides a closer and fuller look at five of the nonwar communities on whose experience Part 1 is based. Part 3 then concludes the book with a chapter that gathers the learning and applies it more generally to other times and places. We address here the basic questions of the book: What is the relevance of the experiences of these nonwar communities to the larger international conflict prevention community? What may be learned and adapted from these examples that will enable us to become more effective and more constructive in preventing conflicts in the future?

Hypotheses About How These Communities Avoided War

Although we are always mindful that implicit hypotheses can misshape findings when observers look for what they expect to find, the individuals involved in gathering the stories of these communities did discuss and imagine some of the factors that might allow these communities to stay out of war. Some suggested that the explanation would lie in the fact that the communities were marginal to the conflict. Either they were remote and in areas where there was little or no military activity, or they were not strategically important to the cause of the war. Some imagined that these communities would have unusually visionary and charismatic leaders who led them to develop unfamiliar strategies and techniques. Others imagined that these communities had been able to "stay below the radar" and avoid attention—partly because they were not strategically important but also because they marginalized themselves.

None of these ideas proved true. In fact, as the evidence will show, each of these notions was strikingly wrong. These communities were located in the midst of fighting and had strategic importance; all of the leadership structures were in place before the conflict and bore strong similarities to those of surrounding communities; and far from hiding, these communities took steps to engage with armies and to interact with them on their own terms rather than those of the war. The surprises were many and instructive.

Terminology Going Forward

This book is about communities who develop strategies to avoid engaging in violent conflict. These groups, as all groups everywhere, are not exempt from differences that divide them within and from others, and they clearly experience and cope with significant disagreements. That is, they do not try to avoid all conflict, because they recognize that differences are inevitable and that struggles can be productive. As we describe the strategies that these groups developed, it should be remembered that the term "conflict prevention" refers to their strategies for avoiding *violent* conflict—not all conflict.

It should also be noted that these thirteen communities were neither pacifists nor antiwar activists. All would fight if they felt a war were justified, and many had fought in other wars. In these cases, they simply calculated that the present war made no sense to them. Therefore, it was not a conflict in which they would participate. Most did not try to end the war or to convince others not to join. They did not try to confront fighters about their ideologies or purposes. They set out their own terms for nonengagement and, largely, managed to maintain these terms.

To reflect the pragmatism and nonideological approach of their strategies, we have chosen to use the term "nonwar communities" to describe these groups. They are not, universally, "peace communities," nor even "zones of peace"—terms used elsewhere. They are groups of people who organized themselves to create and maintain their collective nonwar ways of living as a community.

Conflict Prevention or Avoidance?

The nonwar communities described in this book did not prevent all intergroup violence in their countries. To what extent can they then be said to demonstrate strategies for preventing violent conflict? Would it not be more accurate to say that our focus here is on conflict avoidance rather than prevention?

If our interest were only in how people avoided fighting, we would have both a larger—and less instructive—body of experience. Included would be individuals and groups who flee fighting and become refugees or displaced persons. Groups who are remote or isolated geographically or who make themselves unimportant to the purposes of the war, as suggested in our review of implicit hypotheses earlier, would also be discussed. Every neighborhood that maintained friendships across warring lines, every family that lived its commitment to peace, would qualify for analysis. Even the vast number of individuals who, even though war surrounds them, are not themselves active, would qualify. As already noted, even in war, most people do not take an active part. However, even if they do not become active and even if they object to war, most people are not part of an organized, preexisting community that, as a community, decides it will remain separate from war.

The communities described in this book are included here precisely because they acted, with intentionality and planning, to set themselves apart from the agendas of a war, without, at the same time, acting as peace or antiwar activists. They did not move to avoid conflict nor attempt to make themselves irrelevant. They were not hidden from view by remoteness or because of their insignificance in number. A wide number of people, including armed groups, knew about these communities and brought them to our attention because they—those who did participate in war—perceived that these communities had accomplished something special in their nonengagement. They are interesting precisely because they represent preexisting communities who collectively developed strategies for nonparticipation in war when all the pressures and incentives around them seemingly should have pushed them, like most others, to become involved in the conflict.

Though the alternate route they chose was not war prevention, this route does constitute significant prevention of violent conflict. The communities, themselves, did not claim to be models of universal applicability, and we do not make this claim for them. But what we do see in these stories is a strong, coherent body of experience that might provide useful and practical insights for local and international actors who seek to improve the outcomes of current conflict prevention efforts. In this sense, these cases provide grounded evidence of how, in a range of locations and wars, certain communities have successfully engaged in conflict prevention.

The stories show that prevention of violent conflict is doable. Normal people living normal lives have the option to say no to war. Normal leaders in systems that already exist can respond to and support their people in nonengagement. This kind of conflict prevention does not require special training, new leadership, or special funding. It occurs, repeatedly and around the world in different types of conflict, and we can learn from it. This is the premise of our book.

Notes

1. A useful discussion of the range of theories and approaches embedded in the concept of conflict prevention (and its evolution) is found in Lund, "Conflict Prevention."

2. Over the past decade, many of the international policy documents and conflict-related projects conducted with international funding have reflected these approaches. See, for example, Debiel and Fischer, "Crisis Prevention and Conflict Management by the European Union," which traces the development of the European Union's guidelines on crisis prevention. See

also *The DAC Guidelines on Helping Prevent Violent Conflict*, which emphasizes, with some variations, the importance of anticipating the causes of conflict and addressing them by training, economic development, support of good governance, and to some extent mediation. As the OECD Development Advisory Committee (DAC) document says: "Within the overall efforts by the international community to promote peace-building and conflict prevention, development assistance programmes will find their most important role in promoting the democratic stability of societies." Similar approaches can be found in the policy documents of each individual donor country as well. Some international non-governmental organizations also add engagement with local civil society groups to support their analysis of their contexts and development of conflict prevention efforts. Search for Common Ground (Washington, DC) and Interpeace (Geneva, Switzerland) are just two examples of the many organizations that work with local leaders to promote mediation, institution-building, and attitude change.

3. Most international actors express their commitment to work with, and support, local ownership of peacebuilding activities, but many assume that such support involves training people in new attitudes or skills that they do not yet have. There are notable exceptions to this general approach, which can be found in the individual projects of many nongovernmental organizations. The literature on local success stories is also vast, with most of it focused on peacebuilding rather than on conflict prevention. However, because the lines between these endeavors are often blurred, these stories are important in their recognition of indigenous capacities. See, for example, Galama and van Tongeren, *Towards Better Peacebuilding Practice;* and van Tongeren et al., *People Building Peace II*.

4. There are definite trends under way to look for examples such as these. In the more recent conflict assessment tools of donor agencies, note is taken of existing capacities (among actors and in terms of institutions and processes that exist). See, for example, Goodhand, Vaux, and Walker, *Strategic Conflict Assessment*. Also, the Positive Deviance Initiative (Freidman Center, Tufts University) collects evidence "based on the observation that in every community there are certain individuals or groups whose uncommon behaviors and strategies enable them to find better solutions to problems than their peers, while having the same resources in facing similar or worse circumstances" (quoted from www.positivedeviance.org).

5. Some argue that once violence begins in an area, "conflict prevention" is not the right descriptive terminology (see Lund, "Conflict Prevention"). We recognize that we are stretching the concept, but we do so intentionally because of the importance of recognizing the centrality of effective local processes and systems as a basis for any outsider efforts to support prevention.

6. The two staff, Marshall Wallace and Wolfgang Heinrich, were working for the Do No Harm Project of the Collaborative for Development Ac-

tion (later, CDA Collaborative Learning Projects). They were invited by many active humanitarian and development assistance agencies to help them "mainstream" the ideas and approaches of Do No Harm in their fieldwork as well as at their headquarters.

7. Formerly the Collaborative for Development Action.

8. These can be found on the CDA website, www.cdainc.com.

Part 1

Options and Choices for Preventing Violent Conflict

2

Steps on the Path to Preventing Violent Conflict

In the civil wars of countries as diverse as Colombia and Bosnia, Mozambique and Sri Lanka, Rwanda and Afghanistan, some sizable and significant communities did not participate. These nonwar communities refused to adopt the divisions that defined warring parties and they rejected involvement in the violence. They exempted themselves from the agenda of the war that surrounded them.

If such nonparticipation were obvious and easy, more communities would do it and violence might be circumvented or at least have more limited impacts. On the other hand, if such action depended on rare and extraordinary circumstances and personalities, examples would be hard to find and few people would know of such groups.

The reality is that in virtually every conflict in the world there is a village or a region that, somehow, staked out a nonwar stance. People who do take part in these conflicts often talk about these nonwar groups with puzzlement, because they say that they, too, hoped to avoid war. However, they describe how they finally felt they had no choice but to join with the forces that promised to protect them, to preserve the life they valued, or to force the changes they longed for. As they describe the "other community" that did not fight, some also observe that the nonwar community was more successful at preserving the quality of life that they, as war participants, had thought could only be achieved through fighting. The communities that exempt themselves from the agenda of a war, and manage to survive while doing so, intrigue and confound their neighbors. They are recognized

> Throughout the Bosnian war, the city of Tuzla had an army, it suffered direct shelling from Bosnian Serb forces, and it received regular shipments of food and other assistance through the United Nations and nongovernmental organizations. Still, people across Bosnia as well as within Tuzla describe the Tuzlan experience of the war as "nonparticipation." Tuzla earned its nonwar reputation because its citizens, as a community, refused to separate along ethnic lines. Tuzla not only maintained a multiethnic population in defiance of the war's political agenda, but also reinforced its residents' commonalities through celebrations, mutual help, and even institutionalization of interethnic cooperation in the structures and systems of governance. Tuzla is known for having refused to participate in the "agenda" of the war, defined as it was as one of ethnic dominance and division.

as noteworthy, sometimes admired and sometimes disdained, by others who have experienced the divisions and destruction of war.

What does it mean that these groups exempted themselves from the "agenda of the war"? The experiences reported here will show variations and subtleties particular to each circumstance. What can be said about all of the examples included in this book is that, as communities, they assessed the costs and possible benefits of joining forces in the war and the costs and benefits of not participating and made a collective, strategic choice to eschew involvement. In each instance, they calculated that they had a better chance of preserving whatever was most important to them if they kept out of war rather than taking part in it. In this chapter, we begin to explore the stories of these communities by outlining three steps that each of them took to initiate a nonwar stance: predicting the costs of war, calculating options, and choosing a nonwar identity. It is intriguing that these three steps were common to all the examples.

Step 1: Predicting the Costs

All of the nonwar communities considered here are notable in that they collectively predicted that war was coming to them and would directly affect their lives. It may seem strange that this awareness is notable. However, it represents an important contrast with what many other people describe as their expectations toward impending war. Many who live in conflict-prone areas or in areas where wars have occurred say that they could not have imagined it would happen to them. Some even claim that it is better not to acknowledge war. By acknowledging it, they say, one could make conflict more likely or possibly stop trying to resist or prevent its occurrence.[1] But when people refuse to acknowledge that war will affect them and their lives, it appears to leave them unprepared and to result in their acceptance of war's realities by default, if not by intent.

Sarajevo provides a case in point. Many people in Sarajevo said that because the city had a long history of multiethnic cooperation and because of its cosmopolitan character and fame as host to the 1984 Winter Olympics, they simply believed they would not fight an ethnic conflict. They did not desire war and they did not intend to take part. In retrospect, many felt that, as a city, they were in "collective denial." Some used the term "naive" to describe their prevailing prewar mood.

By contrast, Tuzlans described the process by which they predicted the direct impact of the war on their city and on their lives.

In Afghanistan, as the Taliban took over more and more of the country and approached the Jaghori district in Ghazni province, the people there saw the need to prepare. They called a shura (the basic local structure for discussing and deciding issues) and 200 leaders and community representatives met for ten days to discuss the situation. During this time, they consulted military commanders and talked with people in their communities, gathering views and eventually bringing everyone to understand and share the decision that they should negotiate to surrender rather than fight the Taliban. This decision reflected the community's commitment to female education and the Jaghori way of worshipping and living. The shura concluded that by not fighting, the people of Jaghori would be more likely to maintain their way of life than if they were to antagonize the Taliban by fighting. As they negotiated with the Taliban, they insisted that they would continue girls' education despite Taliban edicts to the contrary.

They remembered the processes by which their mayor and other metropolitan leaders rallied them around the importance of maintaining their multiethnicity, and they recalled the appeal to their history and their pride as they began to take steps that set them apart from active involvement in the war.

The other nonwar communities considered here also predicted that war would come directly to them. And this process—collectively acknowledging that they needed to be prepared to react to war—seemed to prompt these communities to consider options regarding how they should respond. The act of prediction was a precursor to their ability to collectively imagine and create strategies for nonengagement.

There are wide and interesting variations in how the nonwar communities anticipated war. In Colombia and the Philippines, villages and regions that had been previously displaced by warfare (possibly because they had not anticipated it and prepared themselves to respond) collectively acknowledged the likelihood of repeated displacement. Determined to avoid the cycle, they developed alternative strategies for rejecting the agenda of the war. In Nigeria and Burkina Faso, nonwar communities described their decisions as coming from their observations of the damage suffered by others around them who did engage in violence. Nonwar communities in Kosovo reported that they had been disillusioned by earlier political involvements and, as a result, pulled back into local traditional modes of interaction to stay apart from the ethnic divisions that prevailed in other areas. In Mozambique and Sierra Leone, nonwar communities said that they were instructed by ancestral spirits to anticipate how war would affect them and to take steps to avoid involvement.

> In Sierra Leone, as it became more and more apparent to the people of Lawana village that the war would involve them, the imam and the Catholic deacon organized the villagers to pray continuously for seven days. A local official had a dream in which an ancestral spirit of Lawana told him to make sacrifices. He called on the villagers to go into the bush and sacrifice goats, food, wine, and chickens. When they had done so, he had another dream in which he was told that the villagers should return to their homes and that they would be protected from the war.

It could not have been difficult for these communities to predict that war was likely and would directly affect them. However, neighboring communities had the same information and did not, collectively, predict war's impacts on them. Undoubtedly, individuals in other communities did take personal note of the likelihood of war and prepared for it by fleeing to a safer location, stockpiling necessities, or adopting some other preparatory strategy. But individual actions, brave as they are, do not add up to conflict prevention. The process of predicting war prompted a collective consideration of options, and it was this that set these communities apart. This collective prediction of the imminence of war was the common first step taken by the nonwar communities.

Step 2: Calculating Options

Predicting that fighters would come to their communities and demand allegiance and involvement motivated the nonwar communities to take stock and consider options. In the Jaghori district of Afghanistan, collective recognition that the Taliban was coming prompted a widespread consultation through which leaders and local people discussed and debated their situation and explored possible responses. Together they assessed what would be involved if they were to engage in the fighting. They calculated probable losses and gains.

It is likely that many communities recognize the potential destructiveness of war and wish they could avoid it. These nonwar communities took their analysis a step further. Even as they determined that the risks of war were too great, they also analyzed the less-often-considered option of not participating in the conflict. They not only analyzed the costs and benefits of engaging in the war but also did so in relation to an analysis of likely costs and benefits of nonengagement. While they all acknowledged that there were costs for nonengagement, they implicitly opened up the possibility of nonparticipation as an option. Once they had weighed its advantages and disadvantages, it remained for them to figure out how they could actually manage it. The very process of considering that, as a group, they might not take part, distinguishes these communities from their neighbors.

In addition, in weighing their options, the nonwar communities largely eschewed ideological arguments. Many described their choice

When the Jaghori community weighed whether to fight the Taliban or negotiate surrender, they listed the following factors favoring negotiation:

- Most other areas had already been conquered or joined the Taliban.
- The Taliban had outside support and weapons, while Jaghori was a remote district with only itself to rely on.
- War in the area would bring destruction and many casualties.
- If the Taliban won, there would be reprisals against the people of Jaghori.
- The Taliban had made a standing offer not to punish people if districts surrendered to them peacefully.
- Because the Taliban leadership was predominantly Pashtun, as were Jaghori's neighbors, fighting might seriously damage communal relations with those neighbors for a long time.

As a community, Jaghori decided which things were most important to them and, together, determined that they would not relinquish these no matter what. They then developed their strategies for holding on to their cultural and communal priorities without fighting even as they were occupied by the Taliban.

of nonengagement and the actions they took to achieve this as simply "prudent."

In warfare, leaders of opposing sides often appeal to and mobilize their followers by referring to grand ideals. They claim to fight for justice or freedom or some other ideal that, they contend, cannot be achieved by any other means. War propaganda is intended and used to reduce nuance and to force a choice between one side or the other. If people refuse to make this choice, they may be seen to waver on important ideals and come under suspicion from their friends and colleagues as disloyal to their own people or, worse, "sympathetic to the enemy." Absolutism and ideological alignment are common in warfare.

The nonwar communities appeared to avoid propaganda and absolutism. Long-term visions—which most had—translated into compromises and tactics that were eminently pragmatic and undogmatic. Commonly, they cited values and principles that underlay their choices, but they also exhibited agility in their readiness to compromise and concede on some points in order to achieve others. Most claimed their motivations were modest and immediate—to maintain economic or social gains—and they all stressed the practicality of their choices given their circumstances.

In Fiji, people explained that they had managed so far to avoid full-scale civil war because they knew that, if they were to let war take over, the regular deployment of Fijian troops in United Nations peacekeeping exercises would cease. This would not only cause hardship for the families of these troops who benefited from UN wages; it would also represent an unwelcome loss of reputation to the entire country. In Nigeria and Burkina Faso, many people said they were "too poor" to risk the losses they might incur if they fought. In the Philippines, some of the nonwar communities described how they came to realize that, if they were to announce themselves as peace zones, they would receive international economic assistance. In Manipur, local leaders said that they decided they had a better chance of keeping the economic gains their communities had achieved if they could find a way to stay out of the conflict.

These reasons for not engaging in war are not entirely convincing. Obviously, poor people often do fight, sometimes because they think this is the only way they can gain economic justice. International reputation is often sacrificed when national politics place groups in opposition to each other to the point of violence. The economic and reputational reasons cited regularly by many people in the nonwar communities do not tell the entire story. However, they do reflect the fact that the vast majority of people in these communities cited practical calculations, rather than ideals or universal principles, as underlying their choice of nonengagement.

The Muslim community in Rwanda was the exception to the pattern of nonideological choice. They explained their refusal to take part in the genocide as arising from the teachings of Islam. They refused engagement because of religious belief and commitment. Nonetheless, as they unfolded their strategies for dealing with the violence, this community also did so in reference to a realistic shared analysis of their circumstances and a clever pragmatism in the choices they made about where and when to act. Even with a strong religious motivation, they took actions that they calculated would

> In Rwanda, knowing that the Interahamwe were coming to search out and kill Tutsi neighbors, some Muslim communities took the initiative to hide them. Having brought threatened Tutsis into their homes, they then dismantled the houses of those who were threatened, inventorying every item removed "down to the last window frame and fork." Once these items were put into safe storage, they then burned down the remainder of the houses and, when the Interahamwe arrived, told them: "We have already killed these people. See, the house is destroyed."

work based on their analysis of the troubled circumstances. Their approaches paralleled those of other nonwar communities in that they were concerned with prudent effectiveness more than with protecting their own ideological purity.

It is important that nonwar communities did their analyses and weighed their options as a community. The shura that was convened in the Jaghori district of Afghanistan was an impressive demonstration of a broadly collective process for decisionmaking and strategy development. The structures and processes employed by the communities differed depending on history, culture, and preexisting systems. However, the broad inclusivity of the processes for doing their context analyses and weighing options also differentiated these communities from their neighbors.

Finally, it should be noted that the decision by nonwar communities not to participate in the fighting did not, in most cases, represent indifference about the outcomes of the war. In some communities, people had a clear preference for one of the fighting groups over the other. Muslims in Rwanda in no way condoned the actions of the Hutus in killing Tutsis. In the Chidenguele district of Mozambique, most in the community felt greater loyalty to the Liberation Front of Mozambique (Frelimo) than to the Mozambican National Resistance (Renamo). In Tuzla and in Kosovo, most would have feared Serb victory, and in Afghanistan, people of Jaghori district did not welcome the rule of the Taliban. In the Philippine villages, the peace communities of Colombia, the Madhu sanctuary in Sri Lanka, the villages of Manipur in India, the village of Lawana in Sierra Leone, and so on, the individuals in the nonwar communities shared the identities of those who fought and therefore had an interest in how victory by one group would affect their future. Even so, people in all these communities calculated that entering the battle on the terms in which it was being waged was counter to their interests.[2]

In the two nationwide examples, Fiji and Burkina Faso, historically deep-seated political divisions and intergroup tensions had resulted in repeated coups d'état that also included intergroup violence. Everyone in these countries shared the identities that prompted these political standoffs. Even so, people collectively stepped back from full-scale civil conflict and chose to reassert an identity that they calculated would support their connectedness over their divisions. In Fiji, many cited a shared commitment to constitutionality as the connector that overrode ethnic differences, and in Burkina Faso, people referred to pride in their multiethnicity and the importance of their national systems for maintaining it as dominant over ethnic dividers.

All of the nonwar communities conveyed the fact that, despite their own preferences or subgroup identities, they would not take part in the battles. Because fighting according to the agenda of the war made no sense to them, they simply exempted themselves.

Step 3: Choosing a Nonwar Identity

The third common step taken by each of the nonwar communities was to select an identity that distinguished them from the divisions of the war and provided a basis for their cohesion under threat.

Labels are important in warfare.[3] They are used to define sides and designate allies and enemies. Tribe, ethnicity, nationality, history, religion, economic status, and belief system labels are invoked to delineate and categorize the "we" and "they" of battle lines. Propaganda regularly reinforces the connotations of these labels, layering the "we" with the weight of goodness and the "they" with that of badness. Leaders of armed factions are strategic in their choice of labels. They select a label that they know emphasizes and reinforces factors that unite their followers, but that also definitively sets them apart from the groups whom they fight.

The nonwar communities also chose an identity that both reinforced their unity internally and communicated their nonwar stance externally. They made a strategic choice in explicitly identifying factors that already were, or could become, things that connected people in the community. These identities were strategic in three dimensions: they explicitly rejected the categories employed by those who were fighting; they were comfortable, familiar, and natural to the community; and they embodied and communicated outward a set of values that the community agreed on.

Explicit Rejection of the Categories of the War

When the war was about subgroup identities, nonwar communities whose members also belonged to these subgroups named another defining label that, they claimed, superseded the dividing categories. In Rwanda, where ethnicity was the divider that drove the genocide, the Muslim community cited religion as their dominant identity. In Tuzla, where ethnicity and religion defined warring groups, Tuzlans chose their identity as citizens of the city over divisive ethnic or religious labels. In the Philippines, Kosovo, Manipur, Sierra Leone, and Sri Lanka, location provided a connecting identity over the divisions

> Many Rwandan Muslims reported they saw themselves not as Hutus, Tutsis, or Twas, but as a fourth ethnic group, because of historical social segregation and discrimination against them and the fact that Islam builds unity around humanity and faith rather than other identity features.
>
> In Tuzla there was a fierce sense of local identity that everyone shared. When Tuzlans were asked about their ethnicity, some responded, "There are only two kinds of people in Tuzla—those who stayed during the war and those who left."
>
> Speaking for the Ukwa in Nigeria, one person said: "While other areas have been mobilizing their people on how to fight the oil companies, in Ukwa we have been sensitizing our people on how to be peaceful. . . . We have made a deliberate and conscious effort to inculcate in our people the value of being peace-loving."
>
> And in Burkina Faso, an elder man reflecting on his society said: "Ethnicity is a source of personal and national pride for us in Burkina. . . . Each person is proud of his or her own ethnicity without looking jealously at what other ethnicities have. . . . We don't want a homogeneous nation. We appreciate our diversity."

of tribal affiliation, ethnicity, political loyalty, or religion. In Afghanistan, Mozambique, Nigeria, and the Colombian villages, tribal or family group constituted the overriding nonwar identity to distinguish the community from the political alliances that drove those wars.

In all cases, the choice of identity for a community that decided to stay apart from war was chosen in relation to the dividers of that war. Understanding the categories that defined the fight, nonwar communities strategically chose an identity that represented a broad, inclusive connector. Further, by announcing an alternative identity as dominant, they signaled to the fighters their nonalignment with the dividing agenda of the war.

Comfort with the Label

The second characteristic that all the nonwar communities ascribed to their unifying identity was its normalcy. The identities they chose were familiar and made sense historically, geographically, and experientially.

Every nonwar community claimed normalcy in their choice of identity. In Sierra Leone, people said: "We did not join the soldiers or

> In Colombia, many of the nonwar communities' identities arose from past experiences of exploitation and abuse. For many years, wealthy operators had expropriated the lands and resources of indigenous groups for their own profit-making enterprises. Indigenous groups had responded with demonstrations, lobbying, and gathering international support around their right to land. In response, and somewhat to the surprise of those who sought to exploit them, national laws were passed to protect the collective ownership of indigenous land.
>
> It was therefore "natural" for these communities to make collective landownership the identity around which they united. Surrounded as they were by government forces and rebel groups, they chose this other, historical and experience-based identity to position themselves as nonpartisan between the two contending forces.

the RUF [Revolutionary United Front] because here we are all one and respect each other . . . it is part of our history and our ancestors." In Nigeria, the Ukwa people described themselves as "peaceful by nature," noting that "traditionally the Ukwa man is a peace-loving somebody."

Even in the Philippines, where people described how they once were hostile and fought each other, they nonetheless claimed that their course as a nonwar community was based in long-standing "good relations in the community" that had only been "disrupted by forces from outside." They asserted a normal past as the basis of their identity rather than the novelty of their nonwar choice.

People in all the nonwar communities emphasized this point. Again and again, they said: "We just acted normally" and "This is just the way we are, we have always been like this." It was important that the identity chosen "felt" right and familiar. They "simply" (their word) asserted an identity that they could interpret as providing a logical basis for not engaging in war at the time.

The emphasis on normalcy seemed to have had two functions. First, the choice of an identity that felt right to everyone did not require that individuals redefine themselves in order to belong to the community. With the exception of the Philippines, they did not adopt new community identities in opposition to war; they did not reinvent themselves to create a new, separating label. The oddness of the decision not to go to war, when all the communities around them were doing so, was interpreted as being true to their past rather than as requiring some new rationale.

Second, the fact that all these communities claimed naturalness in their nonwar identities demonstrated again the contextual pragmatism that motivated them. They chose identities that were known and familiar not only internally but also to the fighters around them. Because their nonwar identities were known and normal, they had an authenticity and familiarity that was recognized, if not welcomed, by the armed groups who would have wanted their allegiance. In some sense, the familiarity of labels meant that they could not be challenged.

Another aspect of the pragmatism that shaped the choice of nonwar labels is more subtle. As they chose an identity to distinguish themselves from the surrounding war, some of the nonwar communities simultaneously referred back to their fighting prowess in previous wars. Perhaps they did so to assure themselves (and others) that

> Mungoi, whose spirit provided the protective force for the nonwar community in Mozambique, was known, in his lifetime, as a strong warrior. Similarly, the ancestral spirit that protected Lawana in Sierra Leone was honored for bravery and swordsmanship. When the Jaghori people discussed whether to fight or to surrender to the Taliban, one of the factors they listed against surrender was that "Jaghori's fighters were proud of their successes in previous battle, including the jihad against the Soviet Union." In Burkina Faso, people noted: "It is true that we are warriors. But we don't need to make war because we know we are strong."

they were not avoiding war out of cowardice but making a real choice to exempt themselves based on a genuine consideration of the option to fight. Pragmatically, however, these references made another point—that although a nonwar community chose not to fight at the time, it was not, in some ideological sense, opposed to all war and all armies; with sufficient provocation, the community might indeed fight. These communities did not condemn all warfare, but simply chose an alternative path in these particular cases. Such a stance may have been less apt to provoke anger or violence from armed groups.

Chosen Collective Values

The third characteristic of the identities chosen by nonwar communities was that, although the identity labels might have seemed to be neutral (for example, location or ethnicity), the communities imbued them with collective values, attitudes, and principles that they wanted to express in contradistinction to the war. The purpose of the labels was to convey to themselves and others that their shared values differentiated them from engagement in the war. These values staked out their positions in relation to the war they were rejecting.

Some examples illustrate how diverse these values were across nonwar communities, but also how deeply felt and articulated they were:

Colombia. "Most important of all . . . is the concept of *dignity*—their commitment to the right of any Colombian not to be expelled from their land nor attacked for staying on it. This perception of collective dignity is undoubtedly a key factor in sustaining the cohesion of the community in the face of so many challenges."

Burkina Faso. "We don't want a homogeneous nation. We appreciate our diversity." "We have the spirit of forgiveness." "Forgiveness is intrinsic. It dates from time immemorial." "Dialogue and exchange are fundamentally anchored in the Burkinabe spirit."

Rwanda. "The first reason Muslims gave for their non-participation was the role of the Islamic faith and the Koran. Three key teachings were most often cited: (1) that the Koran teaches non-violence, where killing one person is a sin equivalent to killing all of humanity; (2) that the Koran teaches not to differentiate based on labels, but rather that all people are equal; and (3) that the Koran teaches to protect the weak, and assist people who are discriminated against."

Sri Lanka. "The displaced felt protected at Madhu because it was a sacred place with a history of providing sanctuary to those in flight. The perception of Madhu as a sanctuary and as sacred ground was commonly held by Sri Lankans of different ethnicities and faiths, but not always for the same reasons. For Catholics and the Catholic Church, Madhu is a centuries-old place of refuge and the Sanctuary of a venerated Icon. . . . [F]or many Buddhists and Hindus, [it] . . . is sacred . . . because it is situated on historically sacred grounds. . . . Others, of all faiths, venerate Madhu because of their beliefs in its powers to heal."

Fiji. "Despite deep divisions along racial/ethnic lines between Indo-Fijian and Indigenous Fijian, meaning that people in both communities tend to follow their ethnic partisan leadership, many people referred to a collective commitment to the rule of law as the value that kept the country from going into full-scale civil war. They noted that even the perpetrators of repeated coups d'état appeal to the courts to confirm the legality of their actions and, when the court finds against them, even their followers agree that the court is right."

* * *

Discussions of peacefulness were not dominant among any of the nonwar communities. The identities they chose were, in general, descriptive (Muslim, Jaghori, Tuzlan, Mungoi's people), most often related to the location where they lived rather than to ideological belief. Having chosen a label that set them apart from the divisions of the war, they then imbued that label with shared values that together they would not relinquish. The repeated expression of these values and principles to which they adhered was important—not to show their superiority to armed groups, but to maintain internal cohesion around the nonwar choice they had made.

Conclusion

Nonwar communities based the calculation of their choices on a realistic analysis of their context. They acknowledged that there were dangers and risks to nonengagement. They accepted the fact that some of their members would likely be killed and that they would find aspects of their lifestyles compromised by the military and political actions that defined the war. But, as communities, they decided that these risks were more acceptable than those of engagement. They organized themselves psychologically and strategically around this calculation of relative risk and managed to maintain cohesion even as they encountered these expected threats. Impressively, each nonwar community took these steps collectively. They did their analysis as a community, they decided together not to fight, and they agreed to a community identity that all felt embodied their principles.

Notes

1. The discussion within communities mirrors to some extent the broader discussions regarding early warning systems. See, for example, "Early Warning and Early Response."

2. The step into the unknown taken by these nonwar communities reverberates with the fourth discipline cited by John Paul Lederach in the introduction (and subsequent chapters) of his book *The Moral Imagination*, which he calls "acceptance of the inherent risk of stepping into the mystery of the unknown that lies beyond the far too familiar landscape of violence" (p. 5).

3. A discussion of the contextual and psychological dimensions of identity selection can be found, for example, in Gross Stein, "Image, Identity, and Conflict Resolution.

3

Maintaining Community Cohesion

The nonwar communities were able to reject involvement in war when others around them felt they had no choice. They believed, and acted on the belief, that they could opt out of war. Where did this sense of efficacy—of the ability to make a choice—come from? How were these communities able to move from the prediction that war would come to a decision not to take part? And, having made that decision, how were they able to sustain it even as they suffered infiltration, occupation, kidnappings, blockades, and violence from armed groups?

The answer to these questions can be found, in large part, by looking at the way these communities managed their governance. The processes and structures of community life required stability and predictability if these communities were to be able to survive under threat. People needed to be assured that the community would function as an entity and that they would not, through some failure of this entity, be left to face the threats without support. In these nonwar communities, the functions and styles of governance were central to their maintenance of community cohesion.

Two aspects of governance emerged in these communities. The first factor was their focus on maintaining at least some functions of normal governance even as these systems broke down in the war-torn areas around them. The second factor was their ability to sustain and even invent new structures and systems by which to consult broadly and decide issues together.

The evidence from these communities about governance reminds us of an important finding made by the Do No Harm Project[1] almost twenty years ago. In a number of countries at war where the project was involved, we asked people what they thought made a government "legitimate"? In all the countries where people responded, they cited three aspects of legitimacy. First, they noted a negative—that any government that commits violence against its own people is illegitimate, and therefore, legitimacy entails some provision of community and personal safety. Second, people said that a legitimate government provides services (schools, healthcare, and roads were most often named). Third, they said that there must be some system or process by which people feel as if they can be heard. This "voice" took different forms in different contexts. For some it involved elections, but others found systems of representative councils or public meetings suitable. Some women said that they felt they could be heard through their husbands, while others said they required separate avenues for expressing themselves. With local variations, these three essentials—not committing violence against the people, providing services, and providing some avenue for popular voice—were universally held in the countries where we asked people about legitimacy.

This learning from the Do No Harm Project was echoed in the strategies developed by the nonwar communities discussed here. In this chapter, we explore how these communities kept some functions of government operating and the importance of this in promoting a sense of nonwar "normalcy" that contributed to community cohesion. In the next chapter, we turn to the systems and styles of governance found among these groups, and look at the ways that leaders and people communicated and interacted and how these were essential to their ability to successfully opt out of war. Of particular interest are the methods they developed for ongoing and inclusive consultation and decisionmaking, as these were fundamental to the maintenance of community trust, and hence cohesion, under threat.

For these communities to decide not to fight was one thing, but sticking to this decision over time and under pressure was quite another. Maintaining community cohesion around a nonwar identity involved regular and continual attention. It was not accomplished by a single action or proclamation; in these communities it was an ongoing process of achievement, perpetuation, and renewal through multiple daily actions. The stories of these nonwar communities show several distinct common approaches in governance that were critical for ongoing cohesion.

Functioning Governance

Underlying the approaches of all the nonwar communities was a recognition of the importance of maintaining some aspects of nonwar "normal" life. As we saw in Chapter 2, the chosen community identity always felt normal and familiar to people rather than new and recently acquired. Similarly, nonwar communities emphasized normalcy through the continuation of government functions. When the national governments of most of these locations (except for Fiji and Burkina Faso) were involved in war, these nonwar localities kept enough governance going to reassure people of community efficacy. The continuity of these systems was one way of providing daily stability and order and, at the same time, exerting their separateness from the surrounding war.

The nonwar communities focused on three functions of governance: provision of services, establishment and enforcement of codes of conduct, and community security.

Provision of Services

When war around them was destroying infrastructure, these communities managed to keep some services intact and functioning, particularly agriculture, schooling, or healthcare. This continuation of government services was important not only because it gave people access to schools, clinics, and markets, but also because it provided stability and reassurance in the midst of surrounding dysfunction. The sense people had that "some things work"—especially when these were no longer working in areas where there was war—provided one foundation to the maintenance of community cohesion.

When most other areas of Mozambique were suffering severe disruptions, with education and health services virtually nonexistent (except as supplied by international nongovernmental organizations) and food in short supply, Chidenguele (Mungoi's area) continued to maintain all the social services of a functioning government.[2] Schools and clinics were open and staffed, roads were in good repair, and agricultural productivity was relatively high. Within the designated borders of the land of the Mungoi people, these aspects of life went on as normal despite the frequent threats of kidnapping and looting. It was reported that looting never occurred within Chidenguele and that, when soldiers entered the area, they literally left their weapons at the border.

Similarly, even as safety was the primary function of the Madhu Sanctuary in Sri Lanka, the fact that other normal services (safe drinking water and sanitation as well as food and shelter for all) were provided also lent a sense of normalcy to life for those who took refuge there. Over many years of pilgrimages, the clergy of Madhu had developed systems for effectively running what amounted to a small city. Their knowledge of how to manage the provision of necessities for normal life to large numbers of people meant that there was an orderliness and regularity to life within the compound that contrasted starkly with life in the war-ravaged villages that surrounded the sanctuary. In Gornji Livoc, a nonwar community in Kosovo, when their electrical transformer blew out and the government failed to replace it, the community collectively organized a fund and replaced it themselves. And in Afghanistan, not only did the Jaghori community manage to maintain education for all, but they also managed to improve other services, for example by establishing electrical cooperatives, even as infrastructure deteriorated elsewhere.

In Burkina Faso, government services were provided in ways that reinforced cohesion of the different ethnic groups and regions of the country. Civil servants such as teachers, healthcare workers, police officers, customs agents, and town prefects were posted to sites throughout the country "randomly." A policewoman originally from the country's south might be posted to the northwest, and a nurse from the central plateau might find himself working in a health clinic in a far northern desert village. Every few years, civil servants were reposted to new sites. "People get to see other parts of the country," said one teacher, "and they learn that people in other parts are not that different from themselves." Further, people noted that since many young civil servants got married in the area of their first posting, this added to the incidence of interethnic marriage and, again, reinforced a sense of connectedness across regions and subgroups.

The peace zones in the Philippines premised their nonwar strategies on the belief that poverty supports conflict and therefore that increased economic welfare would enable them to stay out of the conflict. They focused on strengthening community organizations, agriculture, preschool education, health, and microenterprise. This effort, initiated and supported by nongovernmental organizations, provided the predictable basis of a functioning infrastructure and of cohesive social organization that the communities associated with nonwar self-governance. In the Philippines and elsewhere, "governance" was carried out not by formal government structures but by some mixture of previously existing structures and ad hoc, informal, and invented systems.

Establishment and Enforcement of Codes of Conduct

The nonwar communities required specified behaviors from everyone who lived within them. This contrasted with surrounding areas, where the uncertainties of war often fed into lawlessness or individualized rules. In most of the nonwar communities, codes of conduct were explicit, agreed to, and enforced; they defined rules for interacting both within the community as well as with militaries and other outsiders.

In Colombia, enforcement of a national law that protected collective landownership was the essential government service that held the nonwar communities together. "Law 70" legalized the land rights of Afro-Colombians and gave them—as communities and not as individuals—title to their lands. For individuals to sell or transfer title of their land required agreement of the entire community. People said that collective land titles provided a mechanism as well as a powerful motivation for maintaining community unity.

In the Philippine nonwar communities, codes of conduct provided instructions about how problems that arose between community members were to be handled. Some referred the troubled parties to specific individuals who were named in the codes or to a group of elders or other respected people, and some required a specified process such as dialogue. Community people were thoroughly familiar with the dos and don'ts of their codes and of their own responsibilities in relation to maintaining them. In both the Philippines and Colombia, codes also laid out rules for maintaining the collective safety of the community in relation to armed groups.

> In Sierra Leone, it was said that during Gbowango's time, the village of Lawana had a strong set of bylaws that included hospitality toward strangers, prohibition of slavery, and sacrifices to the ancestors on feast days. If anyone was caught stealing, they had to dance naked in the village.
>
> Everyone in the community as well as outsiders (including internally displaced persons who stayed there only a short time) noted that the village had always been governed well and that no one had ever been turned away. In addition, unlike other villages in the area, Lawana never forced their youths to leave the village.

At the Madhu Sanctuary in Sri Lanka, the United Nations High Commissioner for Refugees (UNHCR) and the clergy agreed that the refugee population who came there were "expected to conform to all of the rules laid down by the clergy in order to help protect the sanctity, peacefulness and orderliness of the Sanctuary." Playing music, dancing, and unapproved commercial activities were prohibited.

Even in Rwanda, where the genocide brought chaos across the country, the Muslim community continued to live by the rules they had long established. Because they were historically marginalized from mainstream politics, they had been allowed by the Rwandan government to develop their own structures for governance. These continued even during the volatile days of the violence. People noted that "social organization and cohesion are part of the Muslim doctrine."

In Fiji, enforcement of constitutional law was said to be the primary mechanism by which Fijians had so far avoided full-scale civil war. Even perpetrators of the country's coups d'état accepted the supreme court's judgment of their legality.

Other nonwar communities relied on incentives to enforce established rules. Many focused particularly on their youth in order to keep them from joining the fighting, because this would have reverberations for the entire community. However, when young men felt they needed to fight to preserve their honor, communities said that they respected this choice but insisted that the youth go elsewhere to fight in order not to implicate the entire community. Respectful expulsion was the final step in rule enforcement for a number of these communities.

Community Security

Governance strategies for maintaining cohesion in nonwar communities included a strong focus on providing some level of collective security. The communities recognized that their choice not to fight entailed risks. They knew that armed groups would threaten them; they acknowledged that some of their members could be drafted, kidnapped, or killed. It was important that they face these threats collectively and develop a system for handling them that would both deliver some safety and, at the same time, support and assert their cohesion.

The communities developed a range of security strategies including warnings, enabling members to escape when there was danger, acting in concert when there could be safety in numbers, and attracting external public pressure to circumscribe the behavior of armed groups. These strategies were integrated into their systems of internal governance and included rules for both individual behavior and organized collective behavior.

In the peace zones of the Philippines, villagers were required to let everyone know if they were aware of strangers staying in the area overnight. If imminent danger meant it was important to leave, the security rules required that everyone be notified (that is, it was for-

> Every family in Lawana kept at least one, and sometimes more, "bush camps" where they could hide for extended periods of time. Having established themselves as a community who welcomed all strangers, the villagers also developed a system of secret knocks to warn each other of danger so they could go hide in their bush camps. They report that when someone gave the signal, everyone would simply wander out their back doors and off into the bush, as if they were not really going anywhere. Bush camps were kept stocked with sufficient goods to enable people to survive as long as necessary.
>
> The community also used secret signals to designate which outsiders (all of whom they welcomed according to their rules of hospitality) they did and did not trust. Those trusted were informed when rumors of possible RUF attacks might come; those not trusted were ignored, avoided, and isolated, with the hope that they might leave.

bidden for Christians to notify only other Christians, and for Muslims to notify only other Muslims). In Manipur, villages maintained rotations of night-guard duty to warn people if combatants approached. Members of some of the nonwar communities were delegated to infiltrate militant groups in order to gain intelligence about their movements and planned attacks.

Some nonwar communities developed protective strategies that did not involve escape. In Afghanistan, the Jaghori community convinced the Taliban's education officer that it was in his interest (since he allowed them to continue education of girls) to warn them when Taliban delegations were coming to visit. When these delegations came, the community did not stop girls' education but collectively hid the fact that they were defying Taliban rulings. By maintaining collective secrecy about this, the Jaghori community not only avoided Taliban violence but also reinforced their sense of common purpose.

A number of the nonwar communities prohibited weaponry within their borders both to ensure that heightened tensions did not erupt into violence and to demonstrate to external forces that they had no intention of fighting against them. In Madhu, Chidenguele, Manipur, Mindanao, and San José de Apartadó, there were strict rules prohibiting guns within the community. Similarly recognizing that security involved internal community order as well as preparedness for external threats, Tuzlans were proud that they maintained a civilian police force, rather than turning their police into a paramilitary outfit as other cities did.

In Rwanda, the Muslim community was not itself pursued by the Interahamwe. Their security was threatened only when they confronted the militias directly; occasionally, Muslims were killed along with the Tutsis they sought to protect. Although there were times when Muslims risked their own lives, their more common security strategy involved tight community secrecy and trickery to hide the fact that they were assisting Tutsis. When they knew that the Interahamwe were coming, Muslims hid Tutsis by dressing them in headscarves so they appeared to be Muslim women. Many hid Tutsis in backrooms and attics of their houses, moving them across backyard fences and into the hands of other Muslim families if armed militiamen arrived. Such collective secret activities reinforced this community's cohesion as well as its security.

Some nonwar communities pursued safety in numbers. In Colombia, paramilitaries frequently set up roadblocks and check-

However, not all security strategies worked. For example, in one Colombian village, a bell was installed in a strategic location as an alarm to be sounded if an incursion was suspected. The alarm would call the entire population to congregate in the plaza and confront the incursion with the moral force of numbers. If attackers asked to see the village's leaders, the collective response would be to refuse to identify them. But the alarm system was not effective in some cases where the paramilitaries came in too quickly, commando-style, with lots of shooting. After suffering several assassinations and continuous death threats, the villagers used the alarm bell instead as a signal to flee the town center and hide in the hills until the attackers left.

points where individuals were intimidated, disappeared, or killed. By restricting their access to markets, armed groups hoped to strangle economic exchange and force nonwar communities to leave their land. In response, some communities traveled in groups. Facing a desperate lack of goods, one community decided to march en masse to Apartadó to buy goods.

The security aspect of maintaining governance is particularly interesting. It is common for members of military forces to talk about the "solidarity" they feel as they face death together with their fellow soldiers. A similar effect seems to have occurred in these nonwar communities as they also together faced possible death. The mutual trust that was necessary for all Jaghoris to maintain secrecy about girls in school, or for the Muslims in Rwanda to hide and protect Tutsis, united people. The agreement not to provide the names of community leaders under pressure from paramilitaries in Colombia required a level of solidarity and reliability that reinforced mutual trust. In this pursuit of security, the sharing of risks and the processes of developing and adapting strategies for mutual protection contributed significantly to community cohesion.

The Importance of Normalcy

We have seen that an important aspect of governance in these communities was to provide "normal" nonwar services. Codes of conduct and community security strategies also helped these communities maintain a semblance of normal, nonwar life. In the face of surrounding destruction and violence, normalcy was an important factor helping nonwar communities remain united in their decision not to engage in the fighting.

In addition to the serious business of maintaining good governance, nonwar communities also did apparently playful things together. Festivals, sports events, music, and meals—activities that were a part of normal life—were organized specifically to solidify community cohesion. Far from frivolous, such activities affirmed that life was good and allowed the community to enjoy being together. While others around them were divided in the fear and mistrust of war, these communities engaged in group events that asserted the pleasure they took in their own company as yet another demonstration of, and reinforcement to, their confidence that they could trust and rely on each other.

Tuzla. "During the war, celebrations of religious holidays became civil events, celebrated citywide. Celebrations of any sort were important for morale, but also served to bring people together. . . . Everybody became aware of their neighbors' different religions and the holy days they celebrated. . . . An important part of the celebrations were the traditional foods that were cooked. Everybody in a neighborhood would join together to cook the correct food for each holiday, even if it was for another religion."

Manipur. "We knew tensions were running high beneath the surface so we invited the Governor here and during the height of the violence, we had a cultural function with two cultural troupes dancing in the presence of the Governor. Even he was surprised at this. He contributed a thousand rupees to our fund. Then the Manipur Baptist Convention came in and organized an agape (love) feast, and both communities feasted together."

Kosovo. "In Gornji Livoc the village-wide sharing of special events and holidays was not simply something that provided villagers opportunities for enjoyment, but also something they pointed to as bringing them together. One gets the sense that people would have been embarrassed to sponsor an event and not invite all neighbors, regardless of ethnicity. Sharing did not seem to be officially mandated in any way, but rather as a social norm . . . it was considered shameful to host . . . an event and not invite across ethnic lines."

Burkina Faso. "For over 25 years, the government has organized the biennial National Week of Culture. This . . . is the culmination of months' worth of village-level and regional-level dance, theatre, music, cooking, and visual arts competitions. . . . Over the week . . . citizens can see cultural events coming from all over the country, all subsidized by the national government. At just one of the hundreds of events during the week, one might catch performances by a dance troupe from the north, traditional masks from the east, actors from the southwest, singers from the center of the country, and dancers from a neighboring country thrown in for good measure.

"[The] Week of Culture is . . . a potent symbol. . . . The process of recruiting and promoting cultural arts from every corner of the country serves several purposes. In addition to celebrating individual ethnicity's cultures, the event simultaneously exposes members of ethnicities to other cultures. . . . [B]y meeting and singing together and watching each other . . . people get a sense of the 'complementarity' of Burkina's ethnicities."

Rwanda. "People suggested that particularly during this period [Ramadan had occurred only a few weeks before the genocide began], the solidarity within the community as they all performed the ritual of fasting and then breaking the fast together was strong. When the genocide began just a few weeks later, this strong cohesiveness within the Muslim community and the ideals of the Koran were still very present in people's minds."

* * *

Celebration and pleasure were significant in the coherence strategies of many nonwar communities. They had symbolic import, demonstrating both internally and externally the determination of the community to maintain normal life and, pragmatically, lifting morale and providing pleasure in a situation where daily life was difficult in the extreme. In the face of violence and hatred, these communities actively demonstrated the symbolic and the actual closeness of humans who eat and play together.

Not all attempts at normalcy turned out as planned, however. In

Tuzla, an artillery attack from the surrounding area killed seventy young people who were participating in a youth sports event. To honor the dead and affirm the city's solidarity, the mayor designated a common area as the burial site for all who were killed. The city respected the fact that some Muslim families chose to follow their own religious rituals and buried their children in the Muslim cemetery. However, in one Muslim family, when their injured daughter came out of the hospital and found that her parents had not buried her sister in the common site, she urged her parents to move the body to join those of her deceased friends, and they did so. Many people in Tuzla recounted this story as a demonstration of the unity of the city. To change a burial site was seen as a particularly profound recognition of the importance of the symbolic unity.

From outside, the experience of living in the midst of war seems one of constant fear and tension. From within, however, people maintain their humor and find ways to celebrate life with friends and neighbors. Women continue to wear makeup, cook for their families, and teach their children manners. But commonly these exhibitions of normalcy are individually prompted and enjoyed within the immediate family or a small identity group. In contrast, in the nonwar communities, the celebratory side of life was collectively asserted as they continued to eat and play together. Seemingly frivolous fun became integral to their strategies for maintaining community cohesion.

Activities to Assert Peace

We have noted that nonwar communities were not motivated by pacifist convictions and, in general, were not peace advocates. However, they were often aware of their potential impacts on other communities and in some cases did engage in explicit peace activism.

In Colombia, some nonwar villages recruited other villages to disengage from war and worked to develop a broad coalition of nonfighting regions that would add to their individual strength. "The paramilitary strategy destroys the social fabric. So our focus is to sustain our organizational force. . . . We have to strengthen those communities with the capacity to resist and create models that will survive. . . . We also prioritize the formation of alliances . . . we will be meeting with people from other regions to share experiences about how groups have maintained social spaces within the conflict."

In Fiji, after a coup d'état, civil activists organized a number of pro-peace activities such as workshops, discussion groups, and vigils. The Citizen's Constitutional Forum and Human Rights Commission, and, with one exception, Fiji's leaders of mainstream churches, condemned the coup and campaigned to prevent future violence.

In the Philippines and in Manipur, the experience of resisting conflict led some peace zones to take an active role in recruiting others to a peaceful "mind-set" and to extend the geographical areas where fighting would not occur. In some nonwar communities, people said that their status of nonengagement was important because, if they were to succumb to violence, this would cause others to do so too. They saw themselves as modeling an alternative that others could follow.

In Sri Lanka, when the Norwegian-sponsored mediation efforts were beginning between the Liberation Tigers of Tamil Eelam (LTTE) and the Sri Lankan government, the Bishops' Peace, Justice, and Human Development Commission organized a Pilgrimage of Peace throughout the country to engage churches and encourage islandwide prayers and activities for peace. The "Our Lady of Madhu" statue was transported around the countryside on a specially built chariot, and thousands of Sri Lankans of all faiths paid homage to it and listened to the accompanying services for peace. The honor that all faiths gave to this event was based on the years when people from all parts of the country had traveled to Madhu for holidays, healing, or religious purposes.

The lines between refusing to engage in war versus peace activism were sometimes blurred. However, most communities were also careful not to undertake peace activities in ways that demonized fighters or explicitly threatened them. In general, they focused on their own cohesion and survival rather than taking on the broader political arena and the issues underlying the war.

> "In the Kaimai area of Manipur there has been no bloodshed . . . and this example is important for the thirty villages that surround us. Kaimai is like the cap on the bomb, if you lift it up the whole thing explodes. . . . [W]e are not interested only in this village but in the whole area; all Kukis and Nagas are watching this small community."

Conclusion

Analysis of the ways that these nonwar communities maintained their cohesion on a day-to-day basis reveals surprisingly logical and straightforward approaches. All focused on maintaining some limited forms of governance that could provide sufficient reassurance of normalcy to reinforce people's motivation to remain with the community. All focused also on pleasure and the importance of asserting the positive things in life in the midst of severe stress. All showed a flexibility and willingness to adapt strategies to setbacks. These stories from communities who rejected participation in war go some way toward demystifying conflict prevention. The importance of continuing certain aspects of governance and the logic of keeping things as normal as possible both provide possible guidance for steps to be taken elsewhere in the prevention of violent conflict.

Notes

1. Anderson, *Options for Aid in Conflict*, p. 80.
2. We were first alerted to the story of Chidenguele through the fascinating book by Carolyn Nordstrom titled *A Different Kind of War Story*.

4

Leadership, Consultation, and Communication

Important as maintenance of normalcy was, governance in the nonwar communities went far beyond the provision of services, rules of conduct and security. Of even greater importance in their success were the structures of government, which included leadership, consultation, and decision-making. These systems of governance coalesced these communities and provided the infrastructure for collective decisions and unifying strategies.

As noted in Chapter 3, when asked to define "legitimate" governance, many communities said that the possibility for citizens to have a voice was central. People need, they said, to feel that they can be heard and that they are involved in the decisions that affect their lives. As a community made and kept to the decision not to engage in war and assumed the collective risks this choice entailed, a broadly shared sense of involvement was absolutely critical. The nonwar communities described here had systems of governance through which leaders and their members were in continual communication with each other about their status as a group.

In these communities, leadership mattered. But how it mattered challenges prevalent assumptions about the role of leadership in conflict prevention. Many assume that leadership is the key factor that controls whether an effort succeeds or fails. The experience of these communities does not support this belief. The interactions between leaders and communities were more fluid, more iterative, and more complex than a singular emphasis on leadership would imply. Community decisions not to engage in war, their calculation of options, and their processes for maintaining their collective identity did not derive from leadership. Leadership was an important contributor, but not the determinant factor, of processes and outcomes in these communities.

Three widely held assumptions about leaders of nonwar communities are challenged by the evidence. First, many assume that a strong, charismatic leader is necessary to inspire a community to assert peacefulness in the midst of war.[1] If strength and charisma are seen in the leaders who motivate their constituencies to take up war, then it seems logical to assume that these same characteristics must be embodied by nonwar leaders in order to counter the warriors. Embedded in this assumption is another, that peace leaders, similar to leaders of armed groups, operate in a hierarchical framework. In both nonwar communities and armed groups, it is assumed that people need leaders to inspire them to extraordinary acts and that inspiration is delivered from top down.[2]

Instead, we found that leadership in nonwar communities was often multilayered and diffuse, with a variety of roles fulfilled by different leaders at varying levels. In addition, whether there was a single identifiable leader or a multilayered system of leadership, those playing these roles in nonwar communities demonstrated a remarkable openness to ideas, options, and inspiration generated from their constituencies. Leaders encouraged everyone to originate ideas and strategies. They claimed no monopoly on insight, wisdom, or strategic cleverness.

A second commonly held assumption is that to resist violence, people need particular ideologies or visions. Just as military leaders appeal to a set of values that distinguish their followers from the "enemy" and stake out positions of ideological superiority, it is assumed that nonwar leaders must do the same—albeit with alternative values and ideologies. As previously noted, although these nonwar communities did identify certain long-held values that underlay their choices of collective identity, these were assembled and selected to buttress the pragmatic calculation that opting out of war offered advantages over engagement in war. Prior to the articulation of a vision, however, these communities consciously took into account a range of options, including joining the violence. They did not start from an ideological position articulated by a leader.

Third, it is often assumed that the leadership required to enable a community to choose the extraordinary path of conflict prevention must, itself, be out of the ordinary. It is assumed that new and nontraditional leadership and leadership structures are required. With this rationale, a number of conflict prevention strategies focus on training new leaders, introducing new attitudes, and teaching new skills. The nonwar communities examined here showed the opposite. The leadership of these communities already existed and, in the local context, was traditional.

The following discussion is divided into four sections. First, we discuss the characteristics of the leadership in nonwar communities and how communities chose among leaders with different characteristics. Who were these nonwar leaders? Where did they come from? What did people say about them? Second, we discuss the roles that were common to the leadership and examine how these roles both supported and were circumscribed by the roles taken by the larger community. What did these leaders do? Third, we discuss the styles of leadership and how these buttressed collective community strength. How did leaders do what they did and what difference did this make in community cohesion? Finally, we look at the systems and structures of communication between leadership and communities, as these both affected and were affected by the characteristics, roles, and styles of the leadership.

The four sections are clearly overlapping. The characteristics of leaders in some ways determined the roles they took on and were expected to take on. Leadership roles were informed and influenced by the leadership styles. The styles of leadership were directly related to the leaders' characteristics. And leadership characteristics, roles, and styles derived from and reflected the collective community and, in turn, shaped interactions between communities and leaders.

Characteristics of Nonwar Leadership

While the leadership of nonwar communities was always culturally embedded, leaders of these communities shared key characteristics that were relevant to their ability to navigate surrounding conflict.

Preexisting and Embedded

The leadership of these communities that pursued the unusual choice to opt out of war did not emerge only in response to or because of the

"Leadership here [in Nigeria] evolves. You do not just wake up and become a leader. We have a strong and long-standing age grade system which acts as leadership training for us." Because of this, people in Ukwa say that their leadership is trusted, durable, and reliable, and has matured over time.

* * *

In Sierra Leone, the village of Lawana was overseen by a chief, just as in neighboring communities. He had been the chief since before the conflict. He was an "ordinary" leader who nonetheless behaved in ways that allowed or prompted the community to become extraordinary in its choice to stay out of the conflict.

crisis. It was also based in the community's history and identity. In every case, the leadership of the nonwar communities was already in place when the violence began. It was based in traditional local mechanisms so that, in situations where chiefs were traditional leaders, the nonwar communities continued to be led by chiefs, or that, in communities where mayors or councils of elders had traditionally governed, the nonwar communities continued to be led by mayors or councils of elders. In some places, leadership was religious rather than political, as for example in Rwanda, where the imams took the lead, and at the Madhu Sanctuary in Sri Lanka, where the clergy governed. As they took on the risks of choosing not to engage in the war, communities were reassured by this sense of continuity with trusted, experienced leadership. They did not follow new leaders along a new, uncharted course.

However, all previous leaders in these communities were not equal. While it was true that, consistently, nonwar leadership was experienced and known by people, other known and experienced leaders were rejected by nonwar communities because they articulated directions and policies that people did not want to follow. In Rwanda, the Muslim community chose to follow the directions of their imams rather than of the political leaders who were encouraging involvement in the ethnic violence. In Sri Lanka, people chose to move to Madhu, where they knew the leadership maintained a nonwar stance, rather than stay where they were under the guidance of political leaders urging involvement in the war. In Afghanistan, people selected

In Fiji, people described themselves as followers of authority. They also described many layers of leadership—national officeholders, political parties, church authorities and local pastors, local village leaders, and so on. Noting that "the people are more moderate than their leaders," by which they meant the national political leaders, people described how they selectively decided whom to follow each time disruptions occurred. These choices varied over time and were often driven by people's desire to avoid civil war. When any particular leader urged ethnic "loyalty" through violence, most people found another leader to follow based on their own decisions not to participate in the violence.

* * *

Religion was one of a series of factors contributing to the war in Kosovo, and religious leaders often did their part to encourage their congregations to fight. But in Berivojce, "religious leaders were able to have a positive influence" because "that community was receptive to a message of tolerance and patience." This community chose to stay apart from the war and followed individuals who preached peace when others preached war.

their representatives to the shura and reported that when one man, known to be interested only in his own power stood for election, he did not receive a single vote. In Tuzla, those who were not comfort able with the city's nonwar stance left to relocate to other parts of Bosnia or fled, as refugees, to other countries.

In nonwar communities, new leaders were not invented to lead in new directions, but these groups did choose whom to follow from among preexisting leaders. The interaction between communities' choices and leaders' articulation of possibilities was complex and multidirectional. Communities clearly needed leaders to guide them in a nonwar strategy, and many would likely not have imagined this option without a leader. However, when leaders offered the other option of fighting, in these particular communities they were rejected by public will. The dynamic between leaders and communities confounds our attempts to identify who originated the idea of choosing not to engage. Did it come from a leader or from the people? In these nonwar communities, people claimed that it came from both. For example, in

Tuzla, the mayor claimed that he "only did what the people wanted," but the people claimed that "the mayor led us to stay out of the war."

Layered, Shared, Institutional, and Individual

Leadership in nonwar communities was neither rigid nor hierarchical, traits often associated with traditional structures. The very idea of leadership incorporated layers and relationships across layers. In the Philippines, Colombia, and Madhu, individual and local church leaders were important actors, but overall the institution of "the Church" was credited for providing cover and backing for the actions of nonwar communities. Among the Ukwa in Nigeria, there is a clear demarcation of roles so that no one would take it upon himself or herself to lead people into violence without proper consultation. In Fiji, multiple leaders allowed Fijians to choose whom to follow under which circumstances. Such layering of respected and reliable leadership also served as a check on any individual leader. Shared leadership, especially when it came from different levels of society, provided trustworthiness that would have been less possible with a single, identifiable leader.

Layered and shared leadership was also strategic in relation to armed groups. Nonwar communities recognized the vulnerability of having a single leader who could be targeted. Multiple layers and widely shared leadership provided continuity if one or two individual leaders were killed or kidnapped. In Rwanda, when one imam was killed defending people who had taken refuge in his mosque, others continued to maintain the community's refusal to take part in the violence. In the Colombian villages, communities agreed never

> In Manipur, the association of elders and community groups is a force to be reckoned with. Community elders, including all those who are married, thereby making for wide involvement—although pronouncements are usually made by a small, select group of people who are senior in age—help hold the community together. However, the Church acted as a broader unifying force. The Church and community organizations are the two key institutional structures in the Naga and Kuki societies in Manipur.

> Even though Burkina Faso has experienced coups and there is widespread dissatisfaction with politicians, people still say that there will not be any sort of civil strife, because leadership at many levels can work together. "More than anything . . . it is the collaboration of three kinds of leaders—traditional, political and religious—which Burkinabé people see as contributing to the country's ability to avert crises."

to name any individual leader to armed groups who demanded such identification.

Even in the three nonwar areas where an individual leader was prominent and recognized—the mayor in Tuzla, the ancestral spirit of Mungoi in Chidenguele, and the chief in Lawana—leadership roles were shared with and by others. The mayor had a war cabinet who met daily and made decisions together. The spirit of Mungoi was, of course, not vulnerable to targeting by armed groups since he was already dead, but further, his pronouncements were channeled through a medium and interpreted by many who were "possessed" at various times by this spirit. And, even though the chief in Lawana was widely credited with establishing healthy relations that solidified the cohesion in the village, local people also noted that one strength of their chief was the fact that he regularly refused to make decisions for them, instead insisting that they could and should do so for themselves.

In most cases, multilayered leadership was noncompetitive. Only in Fiji did friction among leaders undermine community cohesion. In other areas, leaders seemed to welcome the fact that others shared roles and responsibilities with them. They encouraged broad involvement and accepted that everyone had a role to play.

Roles of Nonwar Leadership

The roles leadership took on were consistent across contexts.

Articulation of Values and Morale Boosting

The leaders of nonwar communities constantly discussed community-held values and related community choices to traditional values.

This articulation of values by the leadership shored up the morale of community members and reminded them that their strategies were grounded in their own valid history. It is hard to imagine how the men of these communities felt, accustomed as they were to protecting themselves and their families from dangers in the mountains of Manipur, the bush of Sierra Leone, or the villages of Colombia, when they agreed to the community decision to surrender their arms. When they were confronted by often-hostile bands of armed fighters, how did they maintain composure and the willpower not to fight? The strategies of nonengagement must have run counter to past notions of what it meant to be protector of one's family or clan.

Therefore, the role of morale-booster was important for helping community members appreciate the strength and courage of their nonwar choice. People needed to be reminded that what they were doing was valuable and important for the entire community and the community's future. They needed to be reminded that the nonwar path was one of integrity and strength, not weakness.

Citing Tradition As the Basis for Nontraditional Choices

Nonwar leadership was always described in terms that emphasized tradition and history. Not only were the leaders in place as leaders because of traditional mechanisms, but they themselves also used tradition to explain nonengagement in the violence. Because they came from traditional systems, they had both the knowledge and the credibility to make use of familiar local histories and symbols to explain and support nonwar choices.

Because of their traditionalism, nonwar leaders could have appeared quite conservative and therefore been nonthreatening to armed groups. Known leadership was familiar leadership. The village

> "It is difficult to overemphasize the role the mayor played in maintaining the morale of the citizens of Tuzla. His indefatigable efforts even earned him a nomination for the Nobel Peace Prize. He was said to have been ubiquitous. He was everywhere, constantly exhorting people to stay cheerful, to not let the enemy win."

> The Jaghori delegations who met with the Taliban to negotiate their surrender pointed out the values they shared: Islamic teachings, that the people of Jaghori district were fellow Muslims living out shared principles and teachings, and that their culture was different, but that it was modest and Islamic.

boys and men who served in the militias recognized and had a history of respecting village councils in the Philippines, Colombia, Manipur, and Kosovo, and tribal chieftains in Sierra Leone, Mozambique, and Nigeria. When these councils and chieftains led the communities in nonengagement, their actions may have been puzzling but not fundamentally strange.

In their ability to connect their community's past and its current nonwar stance by referring to traditional bylaws, the authority of the Quran, local laws, or significant ancestors, these leaders were able to guide nontraditional actions. They called on the past to encourage and promote consideration of new options, both leading their community and reflecting its collective readiness to create options to engagement in the war.

External Articulation of Values and Assumption of Special Risks

Leaders also articulated their nonwar communities' values externally. They were expected by their communities to serve as ambassadors to the outside in negotiating on behalf of their communities and in articulating their nonwar stance beyond their borders. As already noted, often such functions were shared. Groups of Colombian nonwar leaders met with military commanders to secure the release of young community members who had been abducted to serve in the army. The full council of elders in Manipur laid down the rules for behavior to soldiers who came into their villages. Some external functions were deputized by local leaders to a person of "higher" authority. The clergy in the Madhu Sanctuary entrusted meetings with Tamil or government representatives to the bishop. The village leaders in the Philippines enlisted the help of prominent priests to invite army and rebel commanders to their village ceremonies.

Such engagement with the broader environment was sometimes

In Sri Lanka, the bishop remembered one conversation he'd had with a local LTTE commander about attempted recruitment on Madhu Sanctuary grounds. Not accustomed to being dealt with in an assertive way, the commander eventually blustered: "You do not have the right to live." However, the bishop knew that the LTTE had "too much to lose" by alienating the clergy and their flock and therefore they usually respected the limits placed on their behavior.

* * *

The Lawana village chief met with the group and explained that the community had many traditional by-laws and that guns were not allowed in the village. He told them that they would be welcome to stay but they would have to give up their weapons. The chief locked up the weapons and later gave them back to the group when it left. Shortly after they left the village, a man from Lawana who had earlier been captured by the Revolutionary United Front (RUF) to serve as a porter was released and arrived safely at the village.

dangerous. As we shall see in Chapter 5, all the nonwar communities developed strategies for actively engaging with armed groups who were fighting the war around them, and it was the leadership who usually accepted the personal risks of this role.

Functioning Government and Dispute Resolution

Dispute resolution among members of the community was an element of normal governance assigned specifically to leaders. Internal disputes could have proved disastrous for the social cohesion necessary for these communities to resist outside pressures. At the same time, a functioning and fair dispute resolution structure demonstrated social cohesion and inclusivity through its very existence.

Dispute resolution was an expected leadership function precisely because nonwar communities recognized that conflicts would occur among their members, possibly exacerbated by the tensions they faced from the outside. Recognizing that even in their unity, schisms

At the village level in Burkina Faso, conflicts passed through several stages of mediation, each stage being taken care of by a distinct "caste" or group of people defined by their profession. The three castes who intervened as conflict mediators were griots, forgerons, and another group whom interlocutors could not publicly discuss. Griots were village musicians, historians, speechmakers, and diplomats. Their role was hereditary. When conflicts erupted in a village, griots were the first responders. Forgerons represented the next level of mediation. They constructed weapons and farming tools from iron and, because of their mastery of fire, typically commanded respect and fear in a village. Through their connection to ancestors via the forge, forgerons were able to exercise tremendous influence on people who had conflicts. They could ask parties to a conflict to forgive each other. One woman said, "If a forgeron asked you to forgive someone, you have to do so." The third level of mediation was too secret for villagers to discuss, but according to local people it was powerful. Traditional intracommunity and intercommunity mediation mechanisms in Burkina Faso were fundamentally confrontational. The mediators did not speak about finding common ground or establishing similarities between people. Instead, they spoke about the need to emphasize the disputing parties' differences. Indeed, respect for others' worldviews was presented by one griot as a touchstone for peace: "Trying to convince other people of your way of thinking can create conflict."

would develop, they concertedly addressed not only external but also internal problems and risks. Systems and structures for addressing internal differences—not surprisingly rooted in tradition—placed leaders in mediating roles and provided one more mechanism by which they reinforced community cohesion rather than ignoring divisions and allowing them to fester.

Leadership Styles in Nonwar Communities

Leadership styles were inclusive, nonhierarchical, communicative, responsive, receptive, and respectful. Many leaders claimed that,

> In Lawana, the chief led the community with strong traditional values. He had a reputation for being a skilled negotiator so that chiefs in nearby villages came to him for advice. Many people explained that at various points during the war, he presided over disputes involving other villages at the request of other chiefs.

rather than leading, they were themselves being led by the broader community. Leadership was embedded in the communities, and the communities selected and needed their leadership. Leaders were accessible, listening, consultative, and accountable.

Leaders Were Accessible

People in all the nonwar communities felt connected to their leaders. In Chidenguele, anyone was welcome to petition the spirit of Mungoi. The Jaghori shura included representatives from every small village in the district. In Rwanda, the imams met with people in the mosques every Friday and lived among other Muslims. In Manipur and the Philippines, the councils of elders were local and in some cases included men from every family. And in Tuzla, the mayor was seen to be "everywhere."

When people lived in close proximity as they did in Colombia, the Philippines, the Madhu Sanctuary, Kosovo, Lawana, and Manipur, they naturally saw each other and talked with their leaders regularly. In the larger areas such as Jaghori district, the extensive area of Chidenguele, and the city of Tuzla, special systems were devel-

> Anyone could seek help from Mungoi for assistance. For example, a number of people told how if a relative had been kidnapped, you could go to Mungoi and tell the spirit the name of your relative. The spirit would write down the name and immediately your relative would be released and the commanders would have the relative escorted home. You did not need to be native Mozambican to ask for assistance.

> In Burkina Faso, in addition to fostering interdependence, another important social function of joking relationships is to open channels of communication where they might otherwise be closed. This communication reaches the national level. One elder man indicated that because of the joking relationship, he was able to contact the country's president directly to tell him when national policy was negatively affecting the population. This ability to speak freely through joking relationships is one check on power in Burkina Faso and constitutes an important component of the country's social cohesion.

oped to enable regular access and communication between leaders and communities.

In the nation of Burkina Faso, communication was formalized and ritualized through the tradition of "joking relationships." These constitute a well-understood network of ethnicity, family, village, neighborhood, and social class that couples people in relationships that make them responsible for each other's well-being. When people in joking relationships meet, they launch into a litany of mutual insults that follow prescribed patterns and formulas understood by all to express a special bond and the context in which they are related. Many Burkinabés say that joking relationships provide everyone access to the highest leaders in the country.

Beyond the complex networks established through joking relationships, the government of Burkina Faso also created other structures for citizen access to leadership. An Office of the Mediator of Faso was established to "defend the interests of all citizens, no matter what age, gender, ethnicity, or social class" and "to improve the relationship between the state and its citizens." The mediator's delegates, who were mostly retired civil servants who served without pay, were posted throughout the country and were available to everyone free of charge. The mediator herself had direct access to the country's president and she and her staff enjoyed full access to all other parts of government and all government documents.

This sense of access to leadership—whether in a Colombian Afro-Indian village or in the nation-state of Burkina Faso—was common among the members of all the nonwar communities and contributed to their feeling that they had voice in the decisions of the community.

Leaders Were Consultative and Listening

Leaders in all these communities were listening to, and wanted to hear from, the people. Burkina Faso's consultation system was highly ritualized. In all the other communities, though, the consultation systems were less formalized and often involved only face-to-face encounters in the local square (Colombia), on the street (Tuzla), or at the mosque (Rwanda). Often, consultation occurred through representatives (the shura, the council of elders, the medium who channeled Mungoi), but people nonetheless felt they had been heard. In these communities, with the exception of Fiji, where many people felt that they had no connection to what happened at the level of national politics, the systems of channeling ideas and information were seen by community members as responsive and inclusive.

A second aspect of consultation was the flow of information back to the people from the councils or other decisionmaking bodies. In each location (except Fiji), people were able to talk knowledgeably about ideas and options that were considered and the processes

> In Burkina Faso, every Friday morning, the Mogho Naba, chief of the Mossi people, reenacts a ceremony with his five principal subchiefs in a large public square at the center of Ouagadougou. During the course of this ceremony, the Mogho Naba, who begins the ceremony dressed in red, informs the public that he has prepared to enter into battle. His subchiefs, who have consulted the people and know that they do not want to go to war, plead with him one by one, telling him that his people do not wish to go to war. The Mogho Naba leaves, and everyone fears that he has left to launch the battle. However, he soon reappears, wearing any color other than red (typically white), symbolizing that he has chosen to listen to his people and to his subchiefs and not to send the Mossi into war. . . . This weekly ceremony is laden with symbolism. Especially notable is the Mogho Naba's willingness to listen to his subchiefs and, through them, to his people.

> In Afghanistan, during the process of negotiating with the Taliban, the representatives of Jaghori continued to communicate with the people, keeping them well-informed and seeking their views. There was consistent awareness of the operations of the shura, the alternatives facing the population, the key advantages and disadvantages of fighting and surrendering. Different groups, understandably, had different degrees of inside knowledge of the processes and negotiations. Members of the shura, community and religious leaders, military commanders, and members of the negotiating delegations were able to tell the full story, complete with alternatives under consideration at various points. Farmers, women, businessmen, and other ordinary citizens, though generally unaware of the details of the decisions being made, were quite aware of the broader implications of those decisions.

by which decisions were reached, as well as about the specific outcomes of decisions.

In many troubled societies, people talk about information gaps. Some complain that, even though they attend community meetings and voice their concerns, they never hear whether or how their ideas are being considered. But in the nonwar communities, because of the systems developed for ongoing consultation, no one expressed disgruntlement about being left out of or uninformed about decisions that affected the community's nonwar stance.

In many nonwar communities, people said they felt divorced from the national political leadership, describing it as motivated by self-interest and personal power, but they consistently talked familiarly about their own nonwar leaders as people they knew, saw, and interacted with, and as people who listened to them.

Leaders Were Accountable

In most of the nonwar communities, people spoke so admiringly of their leadership and its way of functioning that they felt no need to discuss accountability. However, in several cases, even though the leadership was greatly respected, people did talk about the systems they had for accountability.

In Jaghori, everyone agreed that the quality of the leadership depended on the awareness and participation of the general population. Those who aspire to be leaders depend on the consent of the people. Leaders who broke this social contract were sometimes boycotted or ostracized and eventually forced to resign in disgrace (and when this happened often left the district).

In Fiji, most people cited constitutionality and the rule of law, to which everyone was subject, as the key for accountability. It was important that impunity was impossible at the national—the most divisive—level. In Nigeria, the traditions of the age-grade system were credited with providing restraints on the ability of leaders to act counter to the will of the community. As one person said, this system ensured that "no matter how rich you are, if you are a stubborn somebody [i.e., make decisions without consultation], your mates will tell you to your face."

In Sierra Leone, the greatly admired chief of Lawana actually resigned his position and was replaced because he "violated one of the village bylaws." Again, there was no impunity, even for the strongest man in the village.

A dispute arose in Lawana because the chief loaned one of his acquaintances his still to make local gin. This person kept the still and would not give it back. The brother of the acquaintance was a member of a group of men from a number of villages who had formed a "defense group to provide protection" for the villages from the armies who came to the area. The chief had disapproved of this group and refused to join it, even though he was threatened and beaten for his refusal. When the property dispute arose, the brother returned to the village and beat the chief. Being a proud man and not trusting the "defense group," who he felt had in fact turned on the village and used weapons to exploit rather than protect it, the chief swore on a thunderbox, a strong magical charm from a medicine man. The community reminded him that chiefs were prohibited from swearing, so he resigned his position.

Nonwar Systems and Structures for Communication and Consultation

Because their leaders were accessible, consultative, and accountable, the nonwar communities experienced extraordinary levels of mutual trust that could only be built on broad inclusion in and ownership of all decisions. Clearly the characteristics, roles, and styles of the nonwar leaderships encouraged inclusive involvement and ownership. Beyond that, however, these communities recognized the important role of systems and structures for keeping in touch with each other.

The communication systems and structures developed by the nonwar communities shared three characteristics: they encouraged ideas to come from anyone at any level of society; they systematized a broad consideration of all ideas; and they circulated decisions, once made, to everyone, so that all were continually informed and able to act in accordance with collective decisions.

As mentioned in Chapter 2, someone in the Muslim community in Rwanda originated the idea of burning down houses as a way of convincing the Interahamwe that Tutsis had been killed. Then someone thought of doing an inventory of the contents of the houses and putting these into storage before burning the houses down. Ideas for how to rescue and hide people who were threatened emerged from different people, were improved by others, and then spread across the community.

In Jaghori, meetings were banned because they were seen as threatening to Taliban control. In this district of frequent consultation and discussion of issues, such restriction was a serious problem. For the Jaghori people, the main strategy here was to meet secretly, not to confront the Taliban on this point, but not to lose the tradition of communication and shared decisionmaking.

Jaghoris said that they were better able to resist pressure and prevent confrontation with the Taliban because they had structures and channels to spread information among the populace. When people heard rumors, they knew how to check whether they were true. When new issues or problems arose, people knew how to inform others and generate ideas for how to respond.

During his daily walks around Tuzla, the mayor invited the people he met to come up with ideas for helping the city survive. One resident suggested that music was important for people's morale and noted that there were many musicians still in the city who could form an orchestra. The mayor took this idea back to his war cabinet and, after discussion, they agreed it held promise. One of the cabinet members suggested that the musicians be encouraged to write new songs to reinforce people's sense of common purpose. The idea spread, people got in touch with friends and family who played instruments, and an orchestra was formed and held regular concerts throughout the remainder of the war.

The essential purpose of such sharing of ideas was to encourage collective respect (everyone has good ideas) and to reinforce cohesion (everyone is involved in improving ideas and deciding which to pursue). Dissemination was important for security. When people knew decisions, they could counter rumors that could undermine cohesion. Further, to maintain solidarity—critical to security—everyone needed to know the rules and be informed of strategies.

In one Colombian village, as mentioned in Chapter 3, when the community decided to change the message conveyed by the alarm bell from "everyone gather in the village center" to "run and hide in the hills," it was critical that everyone knew of this change. In Afghanistan, when the Taliban delegations were visiting Jaghori, it was critical that everyone knew how to hide the fact they were flouting Taliban rules.

Some nonwar communities improvised new techniques for maintaining leader-community communication while others simply carried on with what they had always done. The people of Jaghori did some of both—using the shura and its traditional consultative systems when they could and inventing new clandestine strategies when usual meetings were forbidden. Where elder councils existed or towns were small and interconnected by kinship ties, such as in Kosovo and the Manipur villages, communication continued in wartime as it had before, although the content of discussions reflected the challenges these groups now faced. The daily interactions between clergy and residents at the Madhu Sanctuary continued as usual, as did the regular Friday prayer meetings in Rwanda that provided the venue for communication of Muslims with their leaders.

Even though the villages in the Philippines were geographically small, when they decided to become spaces of peace, they developed

> In Nalapaan in Mindanao, a series of workshops was organized as a step toward the community's declaration of the barangay as a "Space for Peace." One of the tasks in the workshops was to draw up a common history of Nalapaan, a process that many felt brought the community closer together than they had been before. The space for dialogue created through these workshops allowed much sharing of stories and ideas that overcame the community's prior divisiveness.

new committees, councils, and meeting places to enable people to discuss and consult across previously dividing lines of ethnicity and religion.

In Tuzla, when the city decided on its course of nonengagement in conflict, the mayor and other members of his administration began their daily walks around the city in order to hear from and talk with people in a new way. In Chidenguele, although Mozambicans often revered ancestral spirits, the possibility of regular contact with the spirit of Mungoi through the medium, on issues related to the conflict, presented a new way of communicating about community decisions and strategies. In a geographical area as large as Burkina Faso, traditional joking relationships continued to provide avenues for broad conversations but, even so, the government developed new venues and systems for top-down, bottom-up communication.

In Colombia, it was the adversity of being displaced by war that led to the development of collective organization. The refugee settings in which these communities found themselves meant that people who seldom crossed paths in their rural homes were in a space where they met daily. It allowed frequent contact between community members, leaders, and external organizations.

Similarly, some of the Philippine communities found that displacement provided the circumstances, albeit unwelcome, for developing closer communication and collective strategies. One reason that the nonwar communities insisted that everyone be alerted if they needed to evacuate was because they recognized that if they moved together and shared displacement, they could use this time to develop shared ideas and improved consultation.

In nonwar communities, the characteristics, roles, and styles of leadership, coupled with communication systems that kept people involved, provided mechanisms for governance that enabled people to have a voice in decisions that affected them. Individually and collectively, leaders not only were open to citizen ideas and opinions, but also actively sought them and encouraged discussion of them. Beyond that, these communities developed structures that enabled the flow of ideas. Good attitudes of leaders without supporting structures would not have been sufficient to maintain community cohesion. Good structures, without accessible, consultative, and accountable leaders, would also likely have failed. It was the integration of these leadership and structural elements that allowed voice and enabled these communities to maintain their cohesion, develop options, and design strategies for nonengagement in war.

Notes

1. For discussion of the role of charisma in leadership and its relationship to context, see, for example, Nye, *The Powers to Lead*. See also Bass, *The Bass Handbook of Leadership: Theory, Research, and Managerial Applications*.

2. See, for example, Gormley-Heenan, "From Protagonist to Pragmatist," for some reflections on elite-driven leadership.

5

Engaging with Armed Groups

Violence breaks out, armies move across an area, militants enter communities looking for recruits and supplies. Fighters are often young men who appear brash and unreasoned, who derive pleasure from the power they hold because of their weapons and who follow commands tenuously. They are wary of disloyalty; they demand allegiance. Civilians are unnerved by their apparent lack of discipline and disregard for human life.

When armed groups surround them, most communities react either by joining the dominant force and accepting its political and military cause (and thus gaining its protection) or by trying to escape notice by appearing passive and unchallenging. The result of either approach is either a willing or a default alignment with the force that is in control of the community's space. Once this occurs, the community is drawn into the war because, seen to side with one force, they become a target for the other. They then are compelled to fight because they cannot risk victory by the other side.

The nonwar communities took a strikingly different, seemingly counterintuitive approach to combatant forces. Recognizing the inevitability that fighters would attempt to conquer and control them, these communities engaged with armed groups. Most of them existed in the midst of two or more fighting groups. Their histories often meant that they favored or identified with one force over others, and everyone—including the armed groups—knew this. Nonetheless, they found ways to exist amid the conflicting groups that satisfied even the sides with whom they deeply disagreed. Because they explicitly set themselves apart from the ideology or agenda that drove the fighting, they were able to stay apart from the conflict.

How did these nonwar communities engage with armed groups without joining them? In this chapter, we explore their inventive strategies for dealing with armed groups while still opting out of war.

Strategies for Dealing with Armed Groups

All of the nonwar communities developed local strategies for engaging with armed groups in their specific circumstances. None of the approaches that were used worked everywhere. None was sufficient by itself. In all cases, communities found it necessary to combine and switch approaches in response to circumstances, adapting or dropping some as they failed in order to develop something more likely to succeed. Not surprisingly, context mattered, and as context changed, strategies also had to change if they were to be effective.

Strategy 1: Nonwar Communities Used Preexisting Networks to Convince Fighters of Their Sincerity

Because the nonwar leaderships had been in place prior to the conflict, they often had personal networks that reached beyond their own communities. In many cases, they used these connections to make contact with militia commanders and warring political leaders. The personal knowledge and trust that they had prior to the conflict became a basis for interaction that, even under war conditions, could still be used to initiate contact.

> The community of Jaghori in Afghanistan wanted to contact the Taliban leadership in advance of the arrival of Taliban occupiers in their district in order to work out arrangements for occupation. "They made contact with old allies who had now joined the Taliban, to reactivate those relationships and get them to act as intermediaries and guarantors. They recognized the need to build trust, so that the Taliban would believe their assurances that no one would kill them."

In Sri Lanka, the clergy of the Madhu shrine and the bishop of Jaffna had, for many years, interacted with senior government officials to make logistical arrangements for the annual pilgrimage to the Madhu Sanctuary, in which thousands of Sri Lankans took part. These prior contacts, focused on disease control, sanitation, and safety, were later put to use when the bishop interacted with the armed groups to ensure that Madhu was exempted from the fighting.

In the Philippines, clergy who had long-standing personal relationships with people in government and with militia heads were able to secure commitment from the Moro Islamic Liberation Front (MILF) and the Armed Forces of the Philippines (AFP) to a "space for peace." In Tuzla, people referred to the mayor's famous telephone call to the commander of the Serbian army unit that resided in Tuzla at the beginning of the war. Because he had a prior relationship with this commander, the mayor was able to persuade him to take his army out of the city.

On the other hand, such networks also existed in Sarajevo—a city with a strong history of multiethnic friendships, cross-group cooperation, and trust. Even though many individuals maintained ties at the personal level, these networks did not keep Sarajevo from becoming embroiled in the conflict. In this, the city was typical of most communities in warring circumstances. Prior connections with leaders of the warring groups did not by themselves support a collective strategy for nonengagement. But where communities had made the collective decision to pursue a nonwar strategy, such connections could be used to establish a level of legitimacy in the eyes of surrounding armies.

Strategy 2: Nonwar Communities Negotiated Directly with Armed Groups on All Sides

Far from staying below the radar, nonwar communities established relations with fighting groups and negotiated with them. Through a proactive approach, they forced combatants to talk to them and thus recognize their nonwarring status.

Nonwar communities recognized that even as they initiated negotiations with armed groups, they did so out of relative weakness. They acknowledged both to themselves and to fighters that they had less power than those who were armed, but they nevertheless insisted on recognition of their right to exist and to set terms for interaction.

In one community in Colombia, the villagers erected a small fence and made a rule that no combatant would be allowed to enter inside it. This simple string of barbed wire on sticks was their basis for "negotiation" with combatants in the area. In spite of the community's injunction, fighters soon crossed this line, ignoring the agreement that the community had hoped to establish. The community responded by announcing that fighters would be allowed inside the fence but that they could not bring weapons across this line. Again, the fighters ignored the community rule and appeared in town carrying their guns. Recognizing their weak position, but maintaining their right to negotiate rules that should be honored, the community then specified that no weapons could be used inside the fence. This condition was met.

Similar to the experience in the Colombian villages, in the Philippines one village that declared itself a "space for peace" noted that it chose the language of "space" rather than "zone" because "in a 'zone' there could be no display of arms and this is a hard one to negotiate with the armed groups and the military, so an easier way was to have a 'space' for peace where everyone was welcome even with arms—the condition being no one could use the arms or have any kind of fight in the space for peace."

One has to ask why these nonwar communities even attempted to negotiate with armed fighters who could and did sometimes threaten and kill them. What did these communities gain through negotiation when they were in a real sense giving in to military dominance? The Jaghori community negotiated their surrender to the Taliban, and the Colombian community simply changed its rule about the boundary each time the combatants violated it. It seemed that these communities usually lost in their negotiations.

The point of negotiation for nonwar communities was not to "win" something but to establish a relationship with the fighting groups. It was the means of initiating interaction and discussing community concerns. The Colombian village that actively set out a negotiating point (the fence as a boundary for weapons), placed itself in relation to the armed groups as a legitimate entity that stood for something. Although the Jaghori community ostensibly surrendered, through negotiation they made clear who they were and how they would and would not interact. When nonwar communities engaged in negotiation with armed groups, it was to force the combatants to implicitly recognize the communities' legitimacy.

In addition, through proactively engaging in negotiation, communities asserted—without appearing to be aggressive—self-respect and equality with the armed groups. Recognition of superior armed power did not signal recognition of any other kind of superiority. By their actions and negotiations, these communities established the fact that they saw themselves as having an equal right to exist on their own terms.

Negotiation was a fundamental part of nonwar communities' strategies for engaging. Through interacting with armies and setting out ideas, boundaries, rules, and roles that they intended to hold, they enjoined the combatants to allow and respect both these roles (which they were willing in fact to compromise) and themselves as human communities (which they were not willing to compromise).

Strategy 3: Nonwar Communities Offered Hospitality for Everyone

Nonwar communities often described themselves as having a "culture of hospitality," a "welcoming tradition," or an "open door" for strangers. A number established themselves as havens of security where everyone was welcome to food and safety. Other groups in countries in conflict may also have had a tradition of hospitality. However, nonwar communities used this aspect of their cultural history strategically to engage with armies and individual combatants.

> The village of Lawana in Sierra Leone did not turn away anyone who sought refuge. Many times the villagers allowed internally displaced persons to stay in their homes and gave them land and seed to farm. Rather than charge outsiders (or in their words, "strangers") for land or seed, they simply shared some of what they had on an individual level, allowing the outsiders to decide if they wanted to give a percentage of the harvest back to the owner. When asked why they did this, they said that it was a part of their history and culture.

Although they talked mostly about providing hospitality for displaced persons, the people in Lawana made a point of not asking who the "strangers" were who came to live with them. They knew that scouts disguised as strangers and other military patrols were among those who visited the community. They knew that the Revolutionary United Front (RUF) was sending scouts to collect intelligence to decide whether to attack particular villages. Looking back, some of the Lawana villagers recounted times when, by showing kindness to all strangers, they convinced an armed group not to attack.

The Madhu Sanctuary in northern Sri Lanka provided another example where the policy of welcoming all comers set the terms by which the area maintained its safety from combat. Madhu restricted all weapons and military recruitment on its grounds, but did not close its doors to anyone who wished to enter. The sanctuary provided shelter, food, and health services without prejudice. Under the protection of the Catholic Church and the United Nations High Commissioner for Refugees (UNHCR), its history of importance to all faiths in Sri Lanka dominated sectarianism so that Tamils and Sinhalese (Muslim, Christian, and Buddhist) were all allowed into the retreat. Warriors were also allowed to enter, but they were expected to abide by the clergy's rules and were evicted if they attempted to recruit within Madhu's boundaries.

In India, several of the peace communities in Manipur reported that they accepted combatants from both sides whenever they came into the village to rest and be fed. In one village, people reported that

The ancestral Spirit of Mungoi welcomed everyone, including soldiers of all sides, to Chidenguele for food, rest, and support. As food became scarce over the war years, army commanders often took the opportunity of returning a kidnapped Mungoi family member when they needed food for their troops. The soldiers who escorted the individuals back to Mungoi were given sufficient supplies for their journey back to their military base. It was therefore in the interests of the armed groups that Chidenguele continue its agricultural production, because, under Mungoi's commitment to "hospitality," the return of kidnapped people provided a mechanism for troop resupply.

soldiers from both Kuki and Naga were in the village at the same time. The "welcome" that was offered to all sides seemed to provide a kind of insurance for these villages. By allowing soldiers to come into their space to live and receive food and shelter—and in particular by allowing soldiers from both sides to do so—the villages maintained a nonaligned stance and gained favor from both sides.

There were, however, problematic aspects to these hospitality policies. In some instances, "hospitality" toward armed groups became "aiding and abetting." In Kosovo, one nonwar community provided clandestine support to the Kosovo fighters and nursed wounded soldiers. Some people claimed that this was in keeping with their hospitality tradition while others noted that they did this because of political preference.

Even though they engaged with armed groups in other ways, some nonwar communities explicitly limited hospitality toward combatants. In Colombia, one community restricted any type of material exchange with armed groups in order not to be seen as supporting them. This community forbade even small shop owners from selling a cold drink to anyone with arms. Shop owners who violated this sanction would be disciplined.

Whether communities pursued a welcoming strategy that involved providing food and shelter to armed groups, or restricted all material interactions, they chose the strategy that they believed would provide the greatest security. For some, sharing increased their chances of survival, while for others, forbidding hospitality better ensured their survival. In either case, communities thought of survival in two senses. First, there was the obvious threat of reprisal from armed groups for some communities if they provided food to the opposing group, such as in Colombia. Second, both choices—to provide hospitality or not—related to community survival in terms of integrity and solidarity. The collective choice was a considered aspect of their strategies for dealing with armed groups.

Strategy 4: Nonwar Communities Confronted Armed Groups

Often, nonwar communities chose to compromise or to appear to compromise with armed groups. This they described as "prudence." However, they also used confrontation as one strategy for engagement. They developed complex push-and-pull, back-and-forth "dances" in which they proceeded in predictable ways for a while and then, forcefully and unexpectedly, challenged an individual or action of a military group.

Many of the stories told about the supernatural powers of Mungoi in Mozambique and of Gbowango in Sierra Leone involved confrontation. One group of rebels who tried to move into Lawana village reported that they met an old man with mystical powers who "diverted" their attention. People said that this old man was the ghost

"When they [the armed group that had kidnapped a member of this Colombian community] were coming through our territory, we knew it right away. Since they were using a vehicle, it was quite easy to block their way, and force them to take the road right through the village. Then we used other vehicles to block their way forward, so they had to stop. We insisted they spend the night in the village. Overnight we roused the entire community, and neighboring communities as well. The next day no one worked, everyone came into the center of the village where we had them. Hundreds of people. We all got there at 6 A.M.

"The four unfortunate guerrillas were completely surrounded by a crowd with machetes and bastones. We crowded them quite close; there was not a chance they were going to draw their weapons. If they did, we said, 'Kill all of us.' This standoff lasted for hours. Meanwhile, the women of the village crowded around Florian, the community member who had been kidnapped, and essentially grabbed him and took him away from the guerrillas.

"Then we opened a dialogue with them. They agreed they had probably made a mistake, but insisted they had orders and had to follow through on them. We told them, 'OK, tell your commandante to come in to the village and we'll talk to him.'

"Later that morning, the Defensor arrived. To pacify the guerrillas, he offered to go with the captain up high on the hill to try to reach his commandante on the phone. We let them go. Then it took them three hours to get the call through, which was pretty suspicious to us. But they came back, with apparent permission from the commandante to admit they had made a mistake and that they could officially release Florian—although we already had him!"

> In Jaghori district in Afghanistan, one religious leader frequently confronted the Taliban leadership, both before they took control and throughout their rule. He reminded them of their responsibilities according to the Quran. He challenged their mullahs to discuss the Quran and Islamic practices, but he was more scholarly than they, and knew more about both Sunni and Shia practices, so they never dared debate him. In part because of him, the district was able to defend its priorities in terms the Taliban found difficult to reject.

of Gbowango. (Although it is not clear whether this is a story of confrontation or negotiation, the fact that it was attributed to a mystical being suggested that it had elements of fright.)

Similarly, the ancestral spirit Mungoi was often reported to have confronted militants. Local people reported how the spirit, when angered, blinded soldiers so they could not see the enemy, sent bees to attack soldiers, and caused a group of soldiers to fall asleep and then told their enemies where to find and attack them. He appeared in these confrontations as a tall man dressed in white, or as a man with a top hat and large gun. He was threatening and challenging. A visitation by a supernatural spirit could not, in either Sierra Leone or Mozambique, be ignored.

Confrontation sometimes involved theological discussions, such as for the Jaghori community in Afghanistan, though effective confrontation did not have to be direct or face-to-face, with Tuzla being an example. In any case, confrontations were not always successful.

In Rwanda, groups of Interahamwe fighters surrounded mosques demanding that Tutsis who had taken shelter there should be turned over to them. When the mullah confronted the soldiers and said, "If you want to kill them, you will have to kill me first," he was then killed. In the Colombian village where people gathered in the town square when the warning bell was rung, several people were killed before they changed strategy. Confrontation was the highest-risk strategy these communities used, and because of this they carefully calculated when to confront and when to back off. They used confrontation sparingly. But because armed groups were accustomed to asserting their power and did not expect unarmed people to challenge them, confrontation could disrupt typical combatant behavior and,

One night the Bosnian Serb army that was camped on the hills above Tuzla lobbed a mortar into the downtown Orthodox church and burned it to the ground. The mayor responded by assigning all city workers to rebuild the cathedral, noting that the church "belongs to all of us." Work went on day and night until the reconstruction was complete. Everyone knew that the army was watching this project from the hill that had been the launch site of the mortar. As electric lights illuminated the cathedral area for nighttime reconstruction work, people in Tuzla showed the army their determination not to be intimidated. They enjoyed the irony that all citizens of Tuzla (Bosnian, Croat, and Serb) worked together to rebuild a Serb holy place that had been destroyed by Serb shells.

when it succeeded, force armed groups to accommodate to the nonwar approach of these communities.

Strategy 5: Nonwar Communities Co-opted Armed Groups

Some nonwar communities "co-opted" fighters by creating situations where a hostile act would entail significant political or military costs for an armed group. The clergy in Madhu, for example, concluded that both the Sri Lankan army and the Liberation Tigers of Tamil Eelam (LTTE) had calculated the political costs and benefits in their decisions about how to interact with the Madhu Sanctuary. When a mortar hit the Madhu church and killed and injured many civilians who had taken refuge there, both armed groups immediately denied responsibility for the attack. Facing strong international criticism for human rights violations, both the government army and the LTTE knew that, were they to be found responsible for the rocket attack, it would be costly in terms of public relations.

Nonwar communities took actions that forced combatant groups to choose whether to take the "moral high ground" or to incur reputational damage. In one town in Colombia, when the army threatened to take up permanent residence in the town center, the community announced that, if the army did so, the entire population would leave. As one town leader said: "If they want the town, they get the whole thing but without us. We won't be victims of their combats on our

> Once a month in Quibdo, Colombia, a boat was loaded with enough goods to restock all community stores. The boat then traveled down the river, with visible international and church accompaniment aboard, delivering supplies to each community. The entire itinerary of the boat trip was announced with complete transparency over the radio in advance. The political cost to an armed group of an attack or robbery against this "Noah's Ark" would have been much higher than an attack against an individual merchant or community.

own land when the others attack." The army calculated that the public relations costs attached to displacing the entire community would be enormous. They did not open their base in the town.

In Jaghori district in Afghanistan, there were many instances of co-optation. When the Taliban refused to accept the Jaghoris' insistence on education for girls, the community co-opted the resident Taliban education officer. Even when Taliban delegations were present, the community had strategies to continue girls' education. Some girls were dressed as boys. Where both primary and high school education were offered, high school girls were sent to primary schools and introduced as teachers. When the Taliban visitors asked about girls' schools, everyone replied that there were none.

The constant negotiation with Taliban representatives on the basis of shared Islamic values and the reasonable, nonviolent strategies that the Jaghori community pursued had an even larger impact on the Taliban than expected. Some Jaghoris reported that "the Taliban arrived as rather brutal, uneducated men, accustomed to dealing harshly with other people. After years of exposure to the courtesy and constructive interactions of the people of Jaghori, they became less brutal."

In the Philippines, nonwar communities invited commanders from all military sides to public ceremonies where they declared themselves as "spaces" or "zones" for peace and signed documents that laid out the terms of their nonwar stance. As witnesses to these declarations and signing ceremonies, both government armies and rebel forces, who were even invited to take part in the festivities that surrounded such ceremonies and share food with villagers, were forced to acknowledge the existence—and legiti-

> In Jaghori, in addition to laying out their own commitment to education and the Islamic support of it, residents also told the Taliban education officer that if schools remained open, people would not kill him and would actually help him build his house. The education officer eventually became an ally and allowed schools to open, provided that they be closed whenever a Taliban delegation was visiting. He also allowed women to be employed as teachers, at a time when all education ceased in some districts because women were not allowed to teach.

macy and seriousness—of these communities. Through such tacit recognition, they became publicly committed to respecting these spaces.

Strategy 6: Nonwar Communities Tricked Armies

In Rwanda, some Muslim communities cut down banana trees and buried them in order to convince the Interahamwe that the mounds were graves of the Tutsis whom they had "already killed." In Manipur, some communities sent young men to enlist in each armed

> Two of the peace communities in Colombia were located quite close to each other, but the terrain was difficult and for a long time, to travel between the two, one had to take a long detour. The communities demanded that the state construct a road to connect them, but this never happened. Finally, the communities built the road themselves, using local materials and without heavy machinery.
>
> As soon as the road was finished, the Revolutionary Armed Forces of Colombia (FARC) took control of it, making it impossible for the two peace communities to use it. When their protests had no effect, the communities made the road impassable on both sides, leaving several FARC vehicles stranded. This finally allowed a more serious negotiation with the FARC and the communities were able to open the road again and use it themselves.

group so that they could gain access to information about troop movements and other military plans.

Among the range of tactics and strategies for engagement with armed groups, trickery was the least often used. In some instances, tricks increased safety (as for Tutsis in Rwanda, villages in Manipur, and the released kidnap victim in Colombia). Other nonwar communities, however, felt that they needed to be completely forthright and honest in order to maintain integrity in their relationships with armed groups. Where trickery was used, it reinforced community spirit, as people enjoyed the fact that, even though they were weaker than armed groups, they could outsmart them. For success, trickery also required that all community members maintain solidarity, which in turn reinforced collective trust.

Conclusion

When nonwar communities "negotiated" with warring groups, they did so not to end the war, but to establish their own legitimacy and space for nonparticipation. When nonwar communities engaged in confrontation, they did so not to build a broad peace movement, but to gain an immediate correction of unacceptable behavior (such as kidnappings and death threats). When nonwar communities co-opted combatant groups, they did not imagine that they would convert them to nonviolence; instead, they intended only to reduce the threats to their continued existence.

The engagement strategies of nonwar communities always had an element of surprise. They did not fit the community behaviors that armed groups were accustomed to—capitulation or quiescence. Unpredicted overtures challenged army commanders and warriors to respond to terms set by the communities and to accept the communities' right to set terms for their nonwar stance. But communities calculated their challenges carefully. Their engagement with armies was both bold and prudent. When a strategy failed to achieve the desired result, communities tried something else. When negotiation failed, they confronted or tricked or co-opted. Using varying and flexible strategies for engagement with armed groups, nonwar communities differed significantly from other communities that hoped to avoid war but were drawn into it.

6

International Involvement and Influence

In all the country cases included here, people told of international influences that had fed into their disunity and subsequent intergroup violence. Still, some of the nonwar communities also described positive international influences and actions that supported their ability to opt out of war.

There were two related layers of commentary. One involved the facts of what happened, when, and by whom. This history was usually directly linked to how things evolved as a sequence of cause and effect. Another layer involved community perceptions of and responses to the history and the facts. What we see from the interactions of these two layers is that, for the nonwar communities, the effects of international actors on them were determined as much by their own responses as by the actual events that involved outsiders.

This is illustrated by the fact that within the same conflict, some people who became involved in the conflict cited colonial divide-and-rule policies as responsible for the divisions that led to their violence, whereas the nonwar communities referred to colonial marginalization as a "blessing" that enabled them to stay apart from political divisions. Whereas some who were involved in a conflict cited international inaction as the cause, the nonwar community claimed that the absence of international influences helped it choose a path of conflict prevention. Whereas in some areas, people cited international meddling as a root of their conflict, nonwar communities encouraged international involvement in their nonengagement strategies.

These differing interpretations of outsider impacts raise challenging questions. To what extent are small, poor, or troubled countries subject to and powerless against negative outside influences, and to what extent can they mitigate these impacts and set their own path? In this chapter we look at how nonwar communities described the help or hindrance of "outsiders" in their strategies for remaining separate from war and explore how in some instances they invited outside involvement and shaped these impacts to support their own nonwar strategies.

Nonwar Communities' Experiences

Fiji

Fiji's colonial legacy was criticized by many for planting the seeds of its intergroup conflict. The British colonial administration had defined Fijians according to race and ethnicity and established administrative and economic systems that resulted in labor stratification and geographic divisions between the groups. When Fiji gained independence in 1970, the national constitution established a system of political representation along the same racial lines, resulting in an almost total political separation of the communities.

> Fijians said that the frequent involvement of Fijian armed forces in United Nations peacekeeping missions kept the Fijian army from getting involved in divisive politics, because if they were seen to support internal violence, they would lose credibility for international peacekeeping efforts. "Smart sanctions" imposed by the international donor community, especially the European Union, the United Kingdom, New Zealand, and Australia, in the aftermath of Fiji's attempted coups, "denied . . . any international legitimacy" to the political aspirations of the coup-planners. International human rights groups and other supportive nongovernmental organizations and trade unions that imposed shipping bans on Fiji when it had a political crisis, and strong Commonwealth and European Union involvement in developing a "clear and coherent road map to ensure that Fiji returned to constitutionality," also supported the return to "normalcy" after intergroup violence.

But this same colonial legacy was also credited for keeping Fiji from going to civil war. Many Fijians thought that the British establishment of constitutionality and the rule of law was the single most important factor in helping them avoid war. Constitutionality was described as a core Fijian value, so much so that one person commented that in Fiji violence was used only to gain power but could not be used to keep it.

Fijian analysts looked upon international influences as both the cause of the divisions that led to violence and the source of the ideas and principles that restrained violence. Both forces were real. Either could become dominant. They noted that the country had repeatedly chosen to rely on the restraining forces when confronted with violence rather than succumbing to the history of division.

Mozambique and Afghanistan

In Mozambique and Afghanistan, Cold War ideologies and struggles were cited by many as the major underlying causes of their violence. However, in Chidenguele in Mozambique, and in Jaghori in Afghanistan, these were seen as irrelevant to the decisions and choices the communities made about their own involvement in the conflict. People in these nonwar communities were as aware as others of impacts of external agendas on their countries. But, recognizing their influence, these communities chose neither to join the ideological battle nor to feel victimized by it, and instead decided to set their own course in relation to the immediate conflict surrounding them.

Nigeria

When asked why they did not take up violence against the oil companies as many others in the Niger Delta did, people in Ukwa mused on the power of propaganda to excite anger. Observing communities around them, they concluded that some international interventions that were focused on achieving justice actually ended up promoting dangerous and counterproductive violence. They decided to reject this kind of outside prompting; they did not want to be directed by what they saw as externally driven campaigns.

Rwanda

In Rwanda, colonialism was again blamed for having codified the divisions between Hutus and Tutsis. The 1994 genocide was, many said, evidence that colonial legacies distort societies through generations in horrendous ways. However, Muslims in Rwanda credited their systematic marginalization under colonialism and subsequently by successive Rwandan governments as a factor that kept them out of the conflict.

The Muslim community had been consistently marginalized from political life and discriminated against in other systems such as education. Under colonialism and even after independence, they were largely confined to live in designated areas. They were exempted from some obligations of citizenship such as labor on public projects, and they were allowed to maintain a separate Islamic political leadership for governing their communities.

This separation translated into the strong sense of community identity that served as the basis for Muslim resistance to the genocide. In retrospect, many pointed to this discrimination as an "advantage" that allowed them to remain apart from the divisive identity-based politics that gripped the rest of the population.

Sierra Leone

Although the failure of international actors to intervene is sometimes criticized as allowing war, Lawana in Sierra Leone saw the lack of international involvement as a plus.

> The village of Lawana is a very self-reliant community that had minimal contact with outside institutions before, during, and after the war in Sierra Leone. This strengthened their identity, sense of community, and ability to maintain "oneness" during the conflict. Rather than relying on others to do things for them, they relied on themselves, reinforcing their own traditional practices.

Tuzla and Sarajevo

Bosnia provides another illustration of the multidirectional influences of international forces on conflicts. In Sarajevo, judgments about international involvement focused on what the international community had not done. A number of people described themselves as "unrealistic" and "naive" because they had believed that the world would not "allow" war to break out in their country, a belief that proved mistaken. They were so sure that the war would not happen that, during the early days of the siege on Sarajevo, many rejected international humanitarian assistance. When their confidence in its restraining force proved wrong, they felt betrayed by the international community that had not lived up to their expectations.

In Tuzla, by contrast, comments about international actors focused on the city's "proud history of resistance" to the Turks, Austrians, and Nazi Germans. This way of recounting their history supported Tuzlans' belief that the city could maintain its separation from broader Bosnian and Serbian political forces. Although throughout the war the United Nations High Commissioner for Refugees (UNHCR) maintained a lifeline of assistance that was critical for the city's survival, not a single resident of Tuzla cited this involvement as an important factor in their decision or in their ability to resist becoming involved in the war.

Sarajevans felt they were compelled to fight because of nonaction by the international community. Tuzlans felt their choices and decisions were their own and not determined by any outside power.

Interventions by International Actors in Support of Nonwar Communities

Some nonwar communities not only insulated themselves against external agendas and impacts, but also invited international involvement and used it to support their own strategies for nonengagement.

Colombia

In Colombia the idea of "peace communities" was first promoted by outsiders—sometimes national, sometimes international. The Catholic Diocese and some nongovernmental organizations (NGOs) approached the communities, suggesting that they become "neutral zones" based on the principles of international humanitarian law.

Although the idea for nonengagement came from outsiders, local people quickly became the originators of the specific approaches and strategies. One part of their strategy was to use the power of international public opinion, buttressed by the outside agencies with which they worked, to co-opt and challenge armed groups.

> In Colombia, most of the discussion of the idea of establishing neutrality took place within the outside organizations that were proposing the strategy. The participation of the population was organized through a series of workshops, mostly attended by community leaders. The more general population was in some cases involved, but primarily in the final ratification stage.

For example, when they threatened to leave their village en masse if the army established a headquarters there, Colombian community leaders counted on their external friends to raise an outcry. They knew their government would be unwilling to face the international pressure that would result if the entire community were displaced at once. Outsider "accompaniment" was also significant in Colombia. An international NGO recruited, trained, and placed individuals from outside Colombia in communities that were under threat, knowing that armed groups were not likely to act against communities when there was an outside witness who could rouse international attention.

The Philippines

While colonial policies had divided Muslims and Christians and subsequent government policies had reinforced these divisions, people in the Philippine nonwar communities relied on, and appreciated, help from outsiders to initiate and maintain their peace zones.

In particular, people talked about charismatic outsiders who personally persuaded communities to declare themselves peace zones. As a "carrot," these outsiders offered material support for local development, followed by programs to help communities discuss their differences and develop trust across ethnic lines. They also used their personal networks to negotiate immunity from attack by warring groups. Frequently, people talked about the inspiration and advice provided by outsiders as essential for their nonwar choice.

The Madhu Sanctuary in Sri Lanka

The Madhu Sanctuary had been a sacred and protected site over many centuries, so it was natural that the area should offer refuge

> The combination of the Catholic Church's religious commitment with the UNHCR's agenda of providing Open Relief Centers was symbiotic and effective. Each reinforced the ability of the other to keep Madhu neutral and provide safety and respite for war-affected people.

from the conflict. The fact that its history and reputation meshed perfectly with the agenda of the UNHCR, which was charged with providing civilian security in Sri Lanka and ending refugee flows from Sri Lanka into India, meant that the two—an established internal sanctuary and a powerful, international institution—merged their interests and were both strengthened by their association.

Both the bishop of Mannar and the UNHCR leadership negotiated military immunity for Madhu. However, the role of the Bishop in maintaining these relationships was more often cited as critical for the safety it achieved than that of UNHCR personnel. This strategy used the UNHCR's international profile to focus an international spotlight on Madhu. In this, it was similar to the strategy used in the Colombian villages and Philippine peace zones, where connections to outsiders supported internal strategies for survival.

When a mortar was fired into Madhu and people were killed, some questioned whether the UN presence made such an attack more likely, or less. Immediately, both armed groups condemned the violence and denied involvement, however, reflecting their calculations that international public opinion, which was focused on the area because of the UNHCR's presence, was critically important. Given this, most people agreed that international involvement heightened security at Madhu more than it jeopardized it.

What Patterns Emerge from These Experiences?

Where international agendas and actions were perceived to have had negative impacts, these often occurred through a colonial legacy that had solidified subgroup identities in opposition to each other. Yet in Rwanda, the Muslim community claimed that marginalization under colonialism helped exempt them from divisive politics. While some claimed that international agendas imposed a conflict-engendering political or military presence, the nonwar communities in Mozambique and Afghanistan demonstrated that these could be made to be irrelevant to local choices. When some, such as in Sarajevo, claimed that the international community let them down by not coming to their aid, people in the village of Lawana felt they were stronger because they had not had undue expectations of the international community and had not become dependent on it. When communities in Colombia and the Philippines welcomed the external promotion of their becoming peace villages, the Ukwa people in the Niger Delta eschewed what they saw as external promotion of an idea of justice that would end by endangering them and their peace.

These differences return us to our original questions: To what extent are local groups powerless in relation to the strong forces of external actors, and to what extent can they either exempt themselves from these or turn them to their own strategic advantage?

There is no doubt that international actors have meddled in others' societies. International agendas, suited to the purposes, interests, and ideologies of international powers, have often played out negatively in others' countries. Even benign agendas have had negative consequences in countries they were intended to help.

However, these experiences and responses of the nonwar communities make it clear that such pernicious impacts did not inevitably determine their choices. Although history shaped the realities these communities faced, it did not leave them powerless. Within the framework bequeathed by a sometimes negative history, people and groups in these communities examined a range of options and chose the ones that suited them. They developed a narrative about their past that reinforced their nonwar choice and invented strategies that sometimes included international actors as important buttresses for these strategies. Most salient in all nonwar communities was their consistent refusal to be victims, either of armed groups that surrounded them or of external powers. The control the nonwar communities exhibited as they interpreted and used their history provides one significant insight into how they shaped their strategies for nonengagement in conflict.

7

From Options to Strategies

In this chapter we bring together the specific experiences of these nonwar communities to suggest a generalizable approach for inventing strategies to prevent violent conflict. The importance of context as these communities developed their strategies cannot be ignored, but looking across these contexts enables us to see important commonalities. And these common strategic elements point to a general approach that may be helpful both for communities that want to step away from conflict in their own locales, and for the international community as it seeks to promote and support the broader prevention of violent conflict.

Step by step, the nonwar communities explored options and marshaled their capacities to develop comprehensive strategies for exempting themselves from surrounding conflicts. Conversations with people from these communities made it clear that, when they took the first step, they did not know where it would lead them. Yet, looking back, they could describe how each successive decision enabled them to imagine the next and, over time, how their choices added up so that they were able to opt out of war.

We begin this chapter by first summarizing the steps taken by these communities that grew into "complete" nonwar strategies, as contrasted with the experiences of surrounding communities that willingly or unwillingly became involved in conflict. From this, we derive an outline of the choices that each community faced and connect these to the capacities that, in their experiences, enabled them to find a nonwar option. Linking options with community capacities enabled these groups to develop their strategies and, therefore, might also be helpful to conflict prevention efforts both of other communities that want to eschew conflict and of the international community as it seeks to promote and support the prevention of violent conflict in its engagements around the world.

Strategies to Survive, Strategies to Win

Overall, nonwar communities sought to live and let live, holding to the principles and lifestyles they felt defined their collective survival, but without trying to impose these on others. Warring communities sought to defeat others and gain dominance for their beliefs and their systems.

Nonwar Communities Anticipated Conflict; Surrounding Communities Did Not

Nonwar communities collectively recognized that war was coming and that it would affect them. Together, members of these communities analyzed their circumstances and made a pragmatic calculation of probable costs to their security and way of life. They then—again as a community—took the unusual step of imagining the option of nonparticipation and, also calculating the costs and benefits of noninvolvement, decided to choose this path.

Surrounding communities sometimes ignored and denied that impending conflict would affect them. Some thought, "It can't happen here." Others did recognize that war was coming and acknowledged its probable costs but felt powerless to do anything about it. Individuals sometimes prepared (by becoming refugees, sending family members to safety, stockpiling supplies, etc.), but these were individual rather than collective actions.

Nonwar Communities Chose an Alternative Identity; Surrounding Communities Adopted the Identities of the Conflict

Nonwar communities chose a collective identity that superseded the dividing identities of the war. In this way, they differentiated themselves, as a community, from the dividing agenda of the conflict. They did not deny that they also had the conflicting identities (Rwandan Muslims were Hutu and Tutsi; Jaghori Afghans opposed Taliban rule; the people of Mungoi favored the Liberation Front of Mozambique [Frelimo] over the Mozambican National Resistance [Renamo]; the citizens of Tuzla were Bosniaks, Serbs, and Croats; and so on). They did not assert their alternative identity as a divider between themselves and others in their country who were engaged in war, but they did select an alternative primary identity (religion, heritage, location) that signaled that they would not take part in the divisions of the war. The collective identity they chose also was one that was familiar and normal, so that it was recognizable as valid both to themselves (i.e., they did not have to take on a new, invented identity) as well as to others around them. And they imbued their chosen identity with a set of values that, they claimed, they had long shared as a community.

Surrounding communities took on the dividing identities of the conflict. They accepted the validity of the label the war applied to them by choosing sides or, minimally, accepting alignment with one side or the other. Although some individuals in these communities recognized that they also had connecting identities with those now defined as "enemies," they accepted the inevitability of partisanship with the side that most closely represented who they were or the politics they preferred.

Nonwar Communities Maintained Services; Surrounding Communities Suffered a Breakdown

Nonwar communities managed, in the midst of war, to provide some level of government services, including keeping schools open; maintaining roads, electricity, agriculture, and other infrastructure; and in some cases providing effective healthcare. Often these services were supported through activities of a combination of ad hoc, nongovernmental organizations and preexisting local government structures.

Surrounding communities often suffered a breakdown in government services. During wars, schools were closed and entire generations of young people were denied education. Roads, electrical grids, water systems, and bridges were destroyed. Agricultural areas were abandoned, markets were disrupted, and food shortages occurred. Many who experience war suffer more from the deterioration of the services of normal life than they do from direct violence. Destruction that occurs during warfare often takes years to rebuild.

Nonwar Communities Maintained Internal Order; Surrounding Communities Suffered Lawlessness

Nonwar communities established codes of conduct that set out the rules of behavior for community members both internally and externally. Internally, such codes usually prohibited the use of weapons or any other action that could disrupt community cohesion, and these communities always provided mechanisms by which disputes between members were to be settled. Nonwar communities were savvy in their recognition that the surrounding tensions would take a toll on their members. Maintaining systems of internal predictable order was therefore seen as one critical function of community governance. Externally, these codes specified how community members were to interact (or not) with armed groups and combatants. While most nonwar communities established policies of openness and hospitality for anyone who entered, the rules by which individual members provided welcome were clear to all.

They had secret codes to communicate with each other, they collectively refused to name individual leaders to outsiders who asked, and they developed systems for warning and hiding when necessary. Their rules provided clarity about individual actions, as these supported and maintained collective identity, cohesion, and security.

Surrounding communities were often subject to lawlessness. Armed gangs threatened and disrupted normal life, and crime often increased. Although armed groups were subject to hierarchical command, at the community level combatant rules were frequently violated. Intimidation through uncertainty was more common than security through regulation.

Nonwar Communities Maintained Internal Security; Surrounding Communities Derived Security from Fighting Forces

Nonwar communities had to find ways to provide security for their members even in the midst of surrounding war. To do so, they relied on their codes of conduct to maintain internal solidarity and on their systems of warning members and providing ways to escape danger. In addition, some found that there was safety in numbers when they traveled together to market or on other errands outside their community. Others developed relationships with groups beyond their borders so that, when they were threatened, they could elicit external support, especially in arousing public opinion to restrain threats from armed groups.

Security strategies were never completely effective. Nonwar community members were sometimes killed or kidnapped. However, the prevailing sense that they were "all in this together" and could entirely trust one another derived in part from their adherence to their codes of conduct, and helped them maintain a sense of greater security than they would otherwise have enjoyed.

Surrounding communities saw their security as tied to the power of the armed group with which they had allied themselves. When this group was dominant, they felt safe. If this changed, the threat rose. When they were located in areas of contention, they sometimes were overrun successively by different armies as territory changed hands. Uncertainty tended to encourage mistrust, even at times of neighbors and former friends.

Nonwar Communities Collectively Celebrated; Surrounding Communities Turned Inward

Nonwar communities consciously organized celebratory events. Their ongoing festivals, banquets, and parties served both to bolster morale and to affirm to the outside world that life goes on despite surrounding war. Nonwar communities also used these events to demonstrate that the things that connected them were stronger than the divisions within the community and beyond its borders. Apparent frivolity served a strategic purpose in supporting community cohesion and conveying a message about the alternative they had chosen to armed groups and others who were involved in war.

Surrounding communities often shrank their common space and ability to enjoy each other. The serious business of survival superseded celebrations and took the time and resources that might have been spent in enjoyment. At the individual level, some families managed to keep their spirits up, honoring birthdays and even laughing together; war zones are well known for their sardonic and biting humor. We even know of instances in which opposing armed groups have met on the sports field or at the beer hall for a "break" from fighting. But the predominant mood in communities at war was sorrowful because of losses they experienced. Many simply maintained a kind of determined grimness to get through the war and hoped that happiness would come later.

Nonwar Communities Shared Leadership and Inclusive Consultation; Surrounding Communities Followed the Leadership of the War

Nonwar community leadership was always traditional; people who held leadership positions were in place before conflict loomed and were trusted because of their familiarity and knowledge of their communities. Where chiefs were prominent in communities, nonwar leaders were chiefs; where mayors governed, nonwar leaders were mayors; where town councils or elders had made decisions, they continued to do so as their communities decided to exempt themselves from war. This said, nonwar communities chose among preexisting leaders, denying allegiance to those who urged fighting and following those who offered the option of nonengagement.

Nonwar community leadership was often multilayered and shared. It was nonhierarchical, consultative, and inclusive, encouraging broad involvement of citizens in consideration of options, discussion of probable costs and benefits of these options, and decisions about the strategies that were chosen. Ideas were welcomed from all sources and communication systems allowed everyone to feel as if they had a voice in decisions. Further, communication systems ensured that everyone was notified of decisions and their rationale so that they all could assume personal responsibility for maintaining community cohesion around these decisions.

In surrounding communities, the war leadership was sometimes traditional and had sometimes existed prior to war, but became known by promulgating an ideology that emphasized differences and divisions among people, thus exciting fear of the "other." Such leaders were characterized by a dominant affect, physical strength (either personal or derived from weapons), and charisma. They used propaganda to reduce nuance, close down discussion, and delineate "acceptable" from "unacceptable" thought. Command structures were hierarchical and subordinates were expected to obey leaders without question. There were few forums for citizens to participate in to consider risks or explore options; communication was top-down and set out rules decided only by those at the top.

Nonwar Communities Engaged with All Armed Groups; Surrounding Communities Allied Themselves with One Armed Group

Nonwar communities and their leaders reached out to and negotiated with armed groups in order to get the combatants to acknowledge the existence and legitimacy of these communities' decisions not to fight. Negotiations were not undertaken to win, but simply to assert their right to exist. Nonwar communities never claimed superiority in either strength or ideology, but did maintain that they had an equal right to live and choose their own course.

Surrounding communities felt forced by the local dominant armed group to avoid contact with other combatants. When armed groups entered into any kind of negotiation, they did so to assert their superiority over others and to win acceptance of their demands. A general rule of fighting groups and the citizens who supported them was nonequality; the enemy was dehumanized and its destruction was portrayed as necessary and legitimate. Disagreement was seen as threatening to the cause and thus was discouraged or disallowed.

Options and Capacities

This review of the strategies of nonwar communities compared to the approaches of communities that were drawn into war illustrates two important characteristics of nonwar strategies—the consideration of options and the reliance on existing community capacities.

Options

The nonwar communities threw off notions of inevitability and powerlessness. When they saw war coming, they imagined as a community not participating. When they reviewed their colonial histories, they imagined ways to turn these to their collective advantage. When they saw the brutality of armed groups that threatened their safety, they imagined collective responses to divert or limit it.

The generation of options rested on anticipation—thinking about what was apt to occur. It required disaggregation—breaking down the all-encompassing problem of war into its definable (and manageable) elements. It required analysis—assessment of the likely costs and benefits of each possible option. And it required confidence in existing collective capacities—what they knew how to do or had the systems to do that would allow them to pursue this option.

Capacities That Connect

The strategies of nonwar communities were grounded in preexisting community capacities. They were based in familiar history and values and in shared experiences and existing systems. The leadership and the communities were able to recognize how what they already had and what they already knew could be relied on as the basis of the extraordinary steps they chose. Rather than inventing new identities, ideologies, or systems, they reaffirmed a collectively held and known identity, they lifted common beliefs above differences, and they invigorated existing structures of communication and governance. The defining characteristic of the capacities they relied on was that they were commonly held. Capacities were connectors, based on shared systems, experiences, values, rituals, economics, and histories. Communities identified connectors in the spheres of life associated with the nonwar options they were pursuing, adapting and modifying them as necessary to maintain internal cohesion as well as to convey their unity of purpose externally. Beyond this, some of the nonwar communities also developed and strengthened strategic connectors to the international world using these links to provide a degree of support and protection for themselves in their decision to stay apart from the war.

Linking Options to Capacities

Although we describe the process by which nonwar communities chose unusual options as a step-by-step one, the actually sequence—once the decision not to fight has been made—can vary widely depending on the context and the challenges that any community faces. Figure 7.1 enumerates these options, though the order is certainly not fixed. In fact, as communities continue to develop nonwar strategies and international agencies work with communities to support the prevention of violent conflict, other steps will undoubtedly emerge. This outline is based on the evidence from the communities studied here, so it is impossible to enumerate all the potential existing capacities for addressing each option.

Figure 7.1 Links Between Options and Capacities in Nonwar Communities

Options	Capacities
Opt out of war	• Decisionmaking systems • Shared or receptive and accountable leadership structures (Societies usually have domineering, hierarchical structures as well as informal, inclusive structures. It is important to identify both.)
Select a nonwar common identity	Range of shared identities: • Historical • Religious • Locational • Organizational
Maintain public services (schools, healthcare, roads, agriculture, etc.)	• Experience • Knowledge • Expertise • Physical assets • Organization
Maintain internal order	• Trusted, respected mediators • Codes of conduct
Maintain security in the presence of armed groups	• Connections to armed commanders • Support from the international community • Communication systems • Hiding places
Enjoy each other, celebrate, boost morale	• Holidays • Feasts • Ceremonies • Culture • Sports • Values

Local context and preexisting experience are fundamental to any collective effort. Our attempt to name capacities that can be brought to bear on the generation of options is, at best, partial and suggestive. However, the categories of capacities are familiar: there are tangible, physical assets; there are organizational systems and expertise; there is knowledge and experience; attitudes, energy, and efficacy underpin positive choices; culture and values connect people.[1]

Lessons to Be Learned

The first and perhaps most important lesson from the experiences of these nonwar communities is that many of the systems, institutions, attitudes, values, and interests that support conflict prevention are already in place and in practice in areas where, nonetheless, conflict exists.[2] When international actors fail to recognize such existing capacities for conflict prevention, they overlook promising opportunities for supporting and strengthening them. When indigenous communities fail to recognize their own such capacities, they can be swayed by divisive leadership or threatened by armed groups to become engaged in warfare even when they recognize it is against their best interests to do so.

The second lesson is that even in war situations, people are not powerless; the choice in conflict situations is not inevitable. When the idea of not fighting was put on the table in each of these communities, normal people and normal leaders were able to generate new ideas and approaches to respond to conflict. In every society, there are leaders who emphasize differences among people as a way to build their leadership, while other leaders emphasize commonalities and connectors. In every society, some communication systems are exclusive and support elites, while others have a broad reach and, to some degree, involve everyone. The cases demonstrate that when options are part of the conversation, communities can make good use of some structures and systems that are available, using them in some cases to take on additional roles, and often bypassing or ignoring those that would inhibit opportunities for finding a different path.

These are the lessons that underlie the validity of the claim that, far more often than is usually imagined, the capacities for conflict prevention already exist in societies—even where there is widespread conflict. Being attentive to this reality and recognizing the importance of considering options and linking them with a conscious survey of existing capacities may enable the pursuit of more generalizable conflict prevention strategies around the world.

Notes

1. In *Rising from the Ashes: Development Strategies in Times of Disaster,* Mary B. Anderson and Peter J. Woodrow list the categories of existing capacities as physical/material, social/organizational, and attitudinal/motivational. In *Do No Harm: How Aid Can Support Peace—or War,* Anderson identifies connectors in systems and institutions; attitudes and actions; values and interests; experiences; and symbols and occasions.

2. Beatrice Pouligny also emphasizes the centrality of existing systems for genuine pursuit of peace in her paper "State-Society Relations and Intangible Dimensions of State Resilience and State Building: A Bottom-Up Perspective."

Part 2

Case Studies of Nonwar Communities

8

Afghanistan: Strategies of Resistance

The Hazara are one of the largest ethnic groups of Afghanistan, living predominately in the central highland called the Hazarajat. There are twenty-four districts in the Hazarajat, and Jaghori is one of the largest. All inhabitants of Jaghori are Hazaras who speak Hazaragi Dari and practice the Shia sect of Islam. The issues of how the population was distributed and in what numbers became highly politicized in two decades of conflict in Afghanistan. However, in the absence of real data, the population of Jaghori was estimated to be about 200,000.

Anticipation of and Preparation for Conflict

In 1997 as the Taliban approached Jaghori, but before they actually tried to take the district, the people there recognized the need to take decisions and to act in anticipation of the probable invasion. As they reflected on why they did this, some people in Jaghori acknowledged that because they were one of the last districts to fall to the Taliban, they had more time than others to anticipate what might happen to them and to consider options, and take preventive action.

This chapter is based on the original case study written in the field by Mohammad Suleman and Sue Williams (see Appendix of Project Case Studies for full reference).

The leaders and community representatives of Jaghori met as a shura (the basic local structure for discussing and deciding issues). There were 200 of them and they met for ten days. During this time, they discussed the situation with each other and, in addition, consulted military commanders and communicated with the population, getting their views, sharing other views they had heard, and eventually bringing the people to understand, accept, and share the decision reached by the shura.

Given what they had seen of Taliban behavior as successive districts joined or were defeated, the people of Jaghori saw only two alternative courses of action for themselves: either fight or negotiate the best deal they could get for surrender. They did not report seriously considering either an outright surrender or fleeing the district. Argued as reasons to fight were:

1. The Hazara had always been discriminated against in Afghanistan, and the Taliban were Pashtun whose culture was very different from that of the Hazara. Given that the Taliban were severely fundamentalist Sunni Muslims determined to force others to follow their practices while the Hazara were Shia Muslims, some felt that the Hazara could only expect rough treatment given their religious beliefs and practices.
2. Many Hazaras had already been killed by the Taliban, though not in this district, and many people hated and feared the Taliban.
3. The Taliban were known to be particularly severe toward women and toward women's education, which was among the highest priorities in Jaghori.
4. Jaghori fighters were proud of their successes in previous battles, including in the jihad against the Soviets, and so were reluctant to surrender.

Argued in favor of surrender, the reasons were:

1. Most other areas had already been conquered or had joined the Taliban.
2. The Taliban had outside support and weapons, while Jaghori was remote with only itself to rely on.
3. War would bring destruction and many casualties.
4. If the Taliban won, there would be reprisals.

5. The Taliban had offered not to punish people who surrendered peacefully.
6. Because the Taliban leadership was predominantly Pashtun, as were Jaghori's neighbors, fighting might seriously damage communal relations for a long time.

In addition, the people of Jaghori were confident of their ability to negotiate and of their solidarity as a community. They had confidence in their leaders to choose a strategy that they could follow. They also believed that because Jaghori was so remote, there would be few Taliban delegations in their area and they would be able to find a way around many restrictions the Taliban would try to impose. And they trusted their Pashtun neighbors, with whom they maintained long-standing, positive relationships.

Negotiating with the Armed Group

The shura decided to be proactive and to negotiate a surrender while preparing for the time to follow. They sent delegations to meet with the Taliban in Kandahar, Kabul, and Ghazni. The strategy of negotiating in all three places simultaneously—Ghazni as the provincial capital, Kabul as the national capital, and Kandahar as the seat of Taliban leadership—was an acknowledgment that the Taliban were not a monolithic nor a strictly hierarchical group, and thus that it would be prudent to get the best agreement possible from all levels of command.

The Jaghori delegations reminded the Taliban of their promise not to punish those who surrendered and of Islamic teachings about the responsibilities of leaders and soldiers toward civilian populations. They pointed out that they shared Islamic values and that the people of Jaghori district were fellow Muslims living out these principles and teachings. They also made some precautionary points. They reminded the Taliban of how much the Russians were hated for their violent behavior. They noted that the district was peaceful and that the people were not fighting among themselves, and pointed out that if the Taliban were not extreme in their rule, the people of the district would be more easily governed and also would not kill them (a thinly veiled threat).

They negotiated not as defeated people but as equals. They initiated negotiations before fighting had come to their area and while the Taliban were still preoccupied with battles in other places. The delegations who did the negotiating in all three areas were instructed to present their values and priorities as standards, not in opposition to what the Taliban might do. Thus they set out their interpretation of Islamic teachings and their commitment to women's education as foundations of their lives.

Continuing Broad Communication and Consultation

During this time, Jaghori's community representatives continued to communicate with their people, keeping them well-informed and getting their views. People reported that they were always aware of the operations of the shura and the alternatives facing the population. They were informed of the calculations of the advantages of surrender relative to the advantages of fighting, and everyone agreed with the decision to negotiate a surrender based on maintaining their way of life.

The shura offered explicit grounds for an agreement. The military units in Jaghori would turn in their arms and return to and be reintegrated into their villages. They promised not to go to war provided that the Taliban would promise not to commit atrocities or interfere in cultural affairs. This was the basis for the settlements with all three levels of the Taliban leadership. The Taliban insisted on limiting girls to primary education, though the shura insisted that this was not acceptable and that the council would continue to negotiate, persuade, and work toward full education.

The people of Jaghori kept their side of the bargain; the Taliban did not. In particular, some Hazaras were tortured or hounded out of the district and there was considerable interference in Hazara cultural affairs.

Taliban Impacts and Jaghori Strategies

Anticipating the destruction they would experience if any of their population did fight the Taliban, the shura developed preventive strategies. When young fighters wanted to battle the Taliban, religious leaders met with them to discourage them. Military commanders had a two-pronged strategy: to discourage them from fighting and to put them to work so they had something to do. If fighters felt that battles were necessary, they were encouraged as they had been during the jihad against the Soviets to take the conflict to the mountains, far from inhabited areas. This was to minimize civilian casualties and destruction of property, as well as prevent Taliban reprisals against Hazara civilians. The shura itself exerted control over people's behavior to make it less likely that the Taliban would punish them. Although some Hazaras were beaten and intimidated, forcing them to leave the area, few were killed. Jaghori was able to hold on to most of its developmental gains and even progress a little, as for example through the establishment of electrical cooperatives.

Resisting Violence, Maintaining Security

The Taliban were well known for their violent treatment of ordinary people who transgressed their many and increasingly restrictive rules. In Jaghori as elsewhere, they beat and publicly humiliated many people. The shura's main strategy to limit this was to encourage people to control their public behavior so as not to come to the attention of the Taliban. At the same time, the council continued to remind the Taliban leaders that extreme behavior would make the district more difficult to govern and potentially make them hated to the point that someone might attack them. Local solidarity meant that, unlike in other areas, most people in Jaghori refused to accept Taliban standards of behavior or punishment, and refused to join, as Taliban leaders urged, in punishing fellow Jaghori citizens.

A women's literacy class in one village did report that Taliban violence resulted in increased and legitimized use of violence in the home. These women reported that their men, after witnessing public beatings and humiliation, would come home and beat them; the women, in turn, would then beat their children. They also reported that this behavior diminished after the Taliban left the district.

Maintaining Commitment to Education Through Negotiation, Co-optation, and Trickery

Even before the arrival of the Taliban, Jaghori delegations presented education as their key priority. It was the one area where they would be prepared to confront and resist restrictions. As elsewhere, the Taliban began with the position that only quranic teachings were necessary. With some difficulty, the Jaghori shura was able to negotiate agreement to allow primary education for both boys and girls, but postprimary education for boys only. Even though the council could not get the Taliban to agree to postprimary education for girls, it continued to insist that this was a high priority for Jaghori.

The key strategy to limit the negative impact of educational restrictions was to build contact with the Taliban's education officer. In addition to laying out their own commitment to education and the Islamic support of it, the shura also told the officer that, if schools remained open, people would not kill him and would help him build his house. It was not clear which of these factors weighed most heavily, but the education officer did become an ally. He eventually allowed schools to open, provided that they were temporarily closed whenever a Taliban delegation was visiting. He also allowed women to be employed as teachers at a time when all education ceased in some districts because women were not allowed to teach. Although most Afghans believed that no girls' high schools were open during the Taliban's rule, such schools were in fact open in Jaghori.

Even when Taliban delegations were present, there were strategies to continue girls' schooling. Some villages offered both primary and high school education, and the residents of these villages would insist that the young girls were students and that the older girls were teachers. Some older girls would be dispersed to primary schools and again introduced to Taliban delegations as teachers. This depended entirely on full community solidarity. When Taliban visitors asked about girls' schools, everyone replied that there were none.

The Taliban also insisted on a "correct" curriculum, limited to approved Islamic teachings. In Jaghori, schools continued to teach science, history, and math as they always had and only when delegations were expected would they use Taliban-approved materials.

It was a risky time to be a teacher, but teachers showed their commitment by continuing in their role as educators even under these circumstances. They did so, they said, because they felt the strong support of the community. Teacher training was completely banned, so experienced teachers assisted younger ones. Occasionally, a teaching seminar would be held in secret. Some villages even found opportunities to send teachers to training seminars in nearby countries. However, this was one area where the Taliban's restrictions were reported to have had real and long-lasting negative impacts in Jaghori.

Throughout this period, there was no outside assistance for education in Jaghori. The Jaghori villages built and repaired schools and provided all materials necessary, with some support from local nongovernmental organizations (NGOs). Their commitment and ability to continue education, even of girls, was the first thing most people mentioned when asked whether Jaghori was different from other districts during the Taliban occupation.

Confronting the Armed Group on Women's Situation

The Taliban were well known for imposing restrictions on women. They justified these as adhering to Islamic practices, although many scholars refuted this. Women everywhere in Afghanistan were confined by the concept of purdah, which meant that they could not be seen by any men other than relatives. The Hazara community, according to the traditional architectural style, contained houses only, with no enclosed compounds, so that the Taliban's restrictions had the effect of limiting women to the interior of their houses. This meant that women had little access to fresh air, sunshine, or social time with other women.

If women went to the local bazaar to buy supplies or tried to continue employment or seek healthcare or other services, they could be severely punished. This had the effect of intimidating most women from attempting to leave their homes. These restrictions were particularly severe for women who lacked male relatives to accompany them. Since the Jaghori district had a high rate of migration of young men seeking work outside Afghanistan, many women were badly affected by these rules.

However, as it became apparent that the community would be warned when official Taliban delegations were expected, many women did continue in their roles as teachers or health workers and left their homes for shopping and errands or to visit doctors. Schools and medical centers continued to employ some women. Women were aware of the risks involved, but knew also that the community supported them and would not inform the Taliban of their prohibited activities.

Elders and community leaders continued their strategy of communication, repeatedly emphasizing to the Taliban that the local culture of Jaghori was different in that it had no tradition of restricting women and saw no justification for it in the Quran. They also reminded the Taliban that everyone suffered if women were unable to go about their usual tasks and that this suffering might cause people to hate the Taliban. They also reminded them that the Taliban had nothing to fear from the unarmed Jaghori population but that even unarmed people could kill them if they were hateful enough.

Additional Security Strategies: Intercommunal Relations

All over Afghanistan, the Taliban exploited ethnic and religious differences to divide and rule. In their early thinking, the members of the Jaghori shura were particularly worried about this. Jaghori is surrounded on three sides by Pashtun groups, and the Hazara and Pashtun had enjoyed good relations, reciprocity, and interdependence for generations. The tradition was that communal conflicts were dealt with by bringing the two sets of elders together. In addition, intractable conflicts within each community were often referred to arbitrators from the other community as trusted neutral parties.

The reluctance of the Jaghori shura to fight the Taliban had partly to do with the perception of their ethnic makeup as largely Pashtun. The Jaghori elders did not want to jeopardize their long-standing good relations with their Pashtun neighbors. To ensure that they maintained these, they made contact with old allies who had now joined the Taliban to seek their assistance as intermediaries and guarantors with the Taliban. They recognized the need to build trust so that the Taliban would believe their assurances that no one would kill them if the Taliban behaved reasonably.

Throughout the Taliban's rule, the Jaghori elders continued to maintain good relations with neighboring Pashtun groups, invoking shared traditions and continuing their pattern of regular meetings. In the first year of their control, the Taliban imposed a blockade on Jaghori, refusing to allow food or essential supplies to pass. Pashtun neighbors came at night to bring food.

Four years later, with coalition forces bombing and Taliban control collapsing, local businessmen agreed to supply money to enable the Pashtun Taliban to return home. In addition, having promised that the Taliban leaders in Jaghori would not be killed, the shura saw to it that they were accompanied home safely.

Maintaining Normalcy: Cultural Affairs

The people of Jaghori district reported that they resisted strongly the pressure to abandon what they saw as their tradition of a peaceful and principled culture when the Taliban tried to impose their violence, humiliation, and self-serving culture. On one level, this resistance occurred internally, as people did not take up the behaviors promoted by the Taliban. At another level, there was considerable pressure on business, administrative, and nongovernmental organizations to engage in bribery and corruption. As one NGO manager reported: "We cooperated where we could, we resisted where we felt we had to, and sometimes we compromised."

One example involved a food-for-work program. The Taliban insisted that they should be exempt from any manual labor but should receive the standard food-for-work rations nonetheless. Local people, who did not think this was fair, negotiated and finally agreed that the Taliban would receive rations for working six hours rather than the standard eight hours. With this agreement, the Taliban were put to work building an administration office for Jaghori—a fact that still brought a smile to the faces of the people of the district.

The Taliban banned meetings of people, which they saw as threatening. In this Jaghori district of frequent consultation and discussion of issues, this restriction was a serious problem. The Jaghori therefore developed ways to meet secretly; they did not confront the Taliban on this point, but they did not compromise their tradition of communication and shared decisionmaking.

In Jaghori as everywhere, music was forbidden. In spite of this, people sometimes played music in their own homes and usually got away with it, though some musicians were publicly beaten and one traditional instrument was "hanged" in the Taliban office. Another strategy was to adapt traditional music to omit the instruments, sing a cappella, and insist that this was their own form of prayer.

There was considerable pressure to close libraries, and many books were burned. Religious leaders both hid books and insisted that the Taliban should support religious scholarship. When one librarian was finally hounded into exile (after being required to report every twenty-four hours to the Taliban's Vice and Virtue Police), the Jaghori community showed its support by keeping the books safely hidden and returning them to the librarian when he was able to return.

The Taliban also interfered in issues of dress and appearance. Women were required to wear the burqa and men the turban, and men's hair and beards were measured and criticized. Although they did not confront the Taliban on adult attire, the community was able to convince the local Taliban administration to look the other way on children's dress. Only when a Taliban delegation was expected were the children required to comply with the rules.

A particular grievance for Jaghori was that their traditional form of greeting between men—an embrace and a kiss on the cheek—was forbidden. Despite considerable negotiation and attempts at persuasion, this continued to be a problem throughout Taliban rule.

Leadership

The people of Jaghori often talked about patterns of leadership rather than about individual leaders. They considered the institution of religious leadership to be a very important factor in their ability to resist Taliban dominance. This covered a range of interventions from persuading young men not to take up arms, to ensuring that the population was well-behaved and therefore less likely to be punished by the Taliban, to making mosques available for girls' schools.

Individual religious leaders were also commended for their courage as well as their scholarship. One such man in particular was cited for having confronted the Taliban leadership both before they took control and throughout their rule. He reminded the Taliban of their responsibilities according to the Quran and challenged their mullahs to discuss the Quran and Islamic practices. But because he was more scholarly than the Taliban mullahs and knew more about both Sunni and Shia practices, they never dared debate him. In part because of him, the Jaghori district was able to defend its priorities in terms the Taliban found difficult to reject.

Everyone agreed that the quality of the Jaghori leadership in general depended on the awareness and participation of the entire population. Those who aspired to be leaders depended on the consent of the people. Sometimes people simply refused to follow a leader, or boycotted or ostracized him so that, eventually, he had to resign in disgrace (and often leave the district). Numerous examples were offered. Particularly interesting were the choices of representatives to the Loya Jirga, the national meeting that eventually selected the post-Taliban government. Military commanders, religious leaders, and political-party leaders from around the country stood for election alongside community leaders. One person said: "Some who wanted to be elected were already discredited. People wanted to throw rotten fruit at them to keep them from standing but we said, 'Let anyone stand and they may not get any votes.' Some were publicly discredited by getting no votes and left the district. We selected eighty representatives, all of them educated people, including elders and women and all kinds of community representatives, and a doctor got the most votes of all."

Channels of Information

Many people of Jaghori noted that, when they heard rumors, they knew how to check whether they were true and were therefore less easily stampeded into emotional reactions. When new issues or problems arose, people knew how to inform others and solicit ideas about how to respond. In the early days of Taliban rule, particularly, Jaghori interlocutors mentioned the importance of everyone knowing what had been negotiated, of monitoring and reporting when the Taliban violated their agreements, and of trusting that problems would be dealt with by their representatives.

When asked to explain Jaghori's relative success at resisting Taliban control, many people from outside the district, even though they were aware of Jaghori's success, could not. However, people inside the district consistently attributed the success to the early meetings, the extensive consultations, and the preventive strategies undertaken collectively. Jaghori was better able to ward off destruction and resist pressure because people were analyzing and reacting to possibilities before they were confronted with actualities. A high level of public awareness, which included women as well as men, enabled the population to stay informed, involved, and united in their strategies. The remarkable level of community solidarity meant that the Taliban were unable to exploit divisions and doubts to manipulate the people.

Case Writers' Analysis

The experience of Jaghori district is important to understanding how communities can prevent conflict and resist strong pressures to change their culture and priorities when others try to force them to do so. It offers a complex, nuanced example of determination and perseverance. This was no starkly heroic or sacrificial stance, although there was a certain heroism in persisting against such unremitting pressures. This was an example of pragmatism as well as principle.

The people of Jaghori did what they could and what they had to in their shared commitment to confront Taliban pressure, particularly on the issue of women's education. In the final analysis, the community was successful. Jaghori did not suffer extensive battle damage or casualties. Girls continued their education. Local structures maintained their authority and their integrity. The Taliban came and went, and the people of Jaghori remained committed to the education of all their children, to Shia Islam, to consultative decisionmaking through the shura, and to good relations with their Pashtun neighbors.

Five key factors explain the success of the Jaghori resistance:

1. The first key to the success of the resistance was its *use of preventive strategies.* The shura council, due to its early awareness, consultations, and decisions, was in a position to negotiate. Strategies were adapted and invented to deal with changing circumstances. Precautions were taken because people continued to hypothesize about possible problems and imagine different ways to deal with a variety of authorities, using different tactics and compromising and persevering.

2. Being strategic depended in turn on *trusted patterns of leadership and participation.* The community's awareness of possible future problems, its shared view of alternatives, and its solidarity in supporting decisions all reflected the traditions of participation and bounded leadership. Everyone understood and accepted the processes of consultation, representation, and decisionmaking. They trusted leaders to carry out responsibilities and they knew what they would do if the leaders turned out not to be trustworthy.

3. The third key element was reliance on *structures already in place.* At the moment when the shura met to consider what to do about the approaching Taliban, it was too late to begin inventing a consultative structure or channels for communication. War disrupts societies, so having access to structures that are already known and functioning was a great advantage.

4. The community also recognized and relied on its *existing skills.* Among the civic, military, and religious leaders and commu-

nity representatives, there were experienced negotiators, community mobilizers, quranic scholars, legal experts, linguists, and cross-cultural interpreters. All of these skills were called upon. The people of Jaghori also recognized what they did not know and called on networks and alliances to gather the information that they felt they needed.

5. Finally and perhaps most important, there were *clear, shared values and principles*. People knew and agreed about what was important and what could be compromised. Ordinary people as well as leaders were aware of the community's priorities and were able to articulate and defend them. On the one hand, this enabled the community to demonstrate the solidarity that was so important. In addition, it bewildered the Taliban, who were accustomed to imposing values on communities that disagreed about what was important.

In many ways, what can be learned from this study of resistance revolves around perceptions. In these circumstances, many people would have perceived themselves to be powerless and indeed many did. Because the people of Jaghori district perceived themselves to have the capability to influence their situation, they looked for and invented alternatives. Because they perceived themselves to be unified, they were. Because they were confident of their ability to negotiate in their own interests, they were strategic in choosing which priorities to emphasize, which battles to fight. Because they perceived themselves to be on a footing of equality with the Taliban, they negotiated as equals. They cooperated where they could, compromised where they had to, and held to their priorities throughout.

In the case writers' interviews with the people of Jaghori, many expressed their appreciation for the opportunity to reflect on this episode in their lives and to come together to identify lessons for the future. As one speaker said, in talking of the jihad against the Soviet invasion: "At that time, we were trained in war, but no one offered to train us in peace. Perhaps we would not have listened; it might have been the wrong time. But we are glad that now we are learning to build peace."

9

Bosnia: Cross-Ethnic Solidarity

The cities of Sarajevo and Tuzla offer an interesting contrast in how responses to violence depend on the sense of options and the support of leadership for exploring those options. In the early 1990s, both cities attempted to reject the violence of the approaching war.

Sarajevo

When they remember the early 1990s, people in Sarajevo tend to describe themselves as "naive" or "in collective denial" regarding the possibility of war ever breaking out in Bosnia. Most people in Sarajevo viewed the war as a reality unfolding in other parts of the former Yugoslavia but not in their area.

In early March 1992, Bosnian Serb paramilitaries barricaded parts of Sarajevo but, in the face of demonstrations by students, were forced to retreat. Bosnian president Alija Izetbegovic said at that time: "Sarajevo will never be blocked in the future. . . . This cannot be repeated in Sarajevo. If it is, we will call on the citizens to stop it, and 200,000 will come out."[1]

One month later, in early April 1992, the Yugoslav army, which was under the direction of Radovan Karadzic and had joined forces

---

This chapter is based on the original case study written in the field by Marshall Wallace and Vasiliki Neofotistos (see Appendix of Project Case Studies for full reference).

with Serbia's president, Slobodan Milosevic, placed barricades in Sarajevo again. In part, the plan was to divide the city along ethnic lines, concentrating Muslims in the old part of Sarajevo and "liberating" the new parts for Serbs.

To protest the division of the city, tens of thousands of local people left their homes and started walking toward the center of the city in a peace march. The response was immediate. Snipers opened fire on the demonstration and killed two people. The march collapsed. The army assumed positions on the hills that surround Sarajevo, prepared to force division upon the city. A few weeks later, demonstrators attempted another peace march. It was attacked as well and collapsed.

Despite the failure of the peace marches to have any effect, people remained in disbelief that war could break out in Bosnia and in Sarajevo. Many blamed external rather than internal forces for the crisis. People finally realized that they were in the midst of war when the siege of Sarajevo started on May 2, 1992, with the blockade of the city. Others reluctantly recognized this reality during the winter when supplies of heat, electricity, water, and food became increasingly scarce.

As a result of this division, many families were split apart, with children who were attending school stranded in one part of the city while parents who were at work were stuck in the other. The barricades were guarded by reservists from Serbia and a mix of locals such as neighbors now dressed in military uniforms. People who were trapped on the wrong side of the city assessed whether their attempt to cross over would be successful based on who was guarding the barricades when they crossed. When neighbors were on duty, people felt that their chances were better than if it were reservists who were the guards.

Identity in Sarajevo

To spread their nationalistic cause, the instigators of armed violence built on, but modified the meaning of, a local notion of "togetherness" that had been a central aspect of Sarajevan life. Whereas the inhabitants of Sarajevo had been proud that they lived together without regard to national affiliation, nationalists propagated an allegedly "better" or "correct" way of thinking that emphasized the "togetherness" of belonging to a Serb, Croat, or Bosniak (Bosnian Muslim) group. Rumors that neighbors of an "other" group would kill "us" began to circulate and these reinforced people's willingness to adopt the new definition of the group within which they were safe. Rumors also stressed the importance of affiliation with one's group lest one become totally socially isolated. As some described it, a "balance of fear" was created among the people, and their resistance to ethnic division was submerged.

People in Sarajevo noted that there were four groups of Sarajevans who took up arms. First were those who did so voluntarily, believing in the superiority of their group over the others. They felt superiority in terms of being "more deserving, more cultured and having a greater history." In describing this group, Sarajevans conventionally viewed them as Serbs who fought against Sarajevo and explained that "killing has always been in their genes." The second group took up arms as a way of defending multiculturalism as it existed in Sarajevo before the war. People later regarded this group as having fought for Sarajevo to prevent the Serbs from imposing their rules. The third group took up arms in response to mistreatment of their loved ones by the army. And finally, a fourth group were forced to fight. That is, they were handed a gun and ordered to join the forces on the hills surrounding the city, and if they refused, they were shot.

Many individuals took great risks on behalf of their friends and neighbors. As the war continued in the countryside, many Bosniaks who had been displaced from their homes fled to Sarajevo. Bosniak old-dwellers who enjoyed a good reputation in Sarajevo (for example, university professors, lawyers, writers, scientists, and people from public life) protected their Serb and Croat friends and neighbors against these Muslim newcomers. Examples included readiness to condemn statements regarding the extermination of the Serb population, insistence on equal distribution of humanitarian assistance, and the protection of life and property. Often, Bosniak old-dwellers stood in the doorways of Serb and Croat apartments and did not allow Muslim refugees to enter and occupy them. Similarly, Serb and Croat old-dwellers who remained in the city protected their Bosniak neighbors and friends against Serb paramilitary units.

Responses to the War

For Sarajevans after the war broke out, survival became the order of the day. People who feared they would not have enough food looted small stores and supermarkets. People burned their flooring, furniture, and other possessions simply to keep warm. Bookstores were also looted as people used books for fuel.

In January 1993, the Bosnian army undertook to construct a tunnel to connect Sarajevo with other parts of Bosnian territory not controlled by the Yugoslav army. Despite shelling and bad weather, the tunnel was completed in July of that year and served a variety of purposes, both military and civilian. The Bosnian army used it to bring arms into the city and to evacuate the injured. In addition, they used it to move out of Sarajevo and position themselves on the hills around the city as a way to combat Serb troops who controlled these areas. Civilians also used the tunnel to bring in supplies. However, profiteers quickly took advantage of the import opportunity afforded by control of the tunnel and some became incredibly wealthy from their ability to exploit it to sell to the isolated and needy city population. Sarajevans said that the Bosnian president Alija Izetbegovic assured them that war would be prevented by Europe. Though they did not remember exact words or speeches, many people said his public pronouncements in early 1992 suggested to them that a diplomatic process was under way to solve the political crises in Yugoslavia. Given also his comments praising the student demonstration of March 4, they said he did not prepare them for what was to follow, and that his statements may have supported their naiveté. Many also remembered that they held out hope for months that international pressure could end the siege and the suffering.

Two years after the start of the war, in 1994, Sarajevo selected a new mayor, Tarik Kupusovic. A hydro-engineer by profession, he said his mandate was "to get services working." Working with other engineers, both Bosnian and foreign, he succeeded to some degree. But he saw his role during the war as limited to technical issues, not political or strategic ones. He was among those who identified the fact that Sarajevo was the capital and therefore that national-level politicians and military commanders had more influence than the mayor.

Aftermath

Looking back, people in Sarajevo emphasized that there had never been fighting among the various ethnic and religious groups throughout a regional history that spanned thousands of years. The war in Bosnia, they said, should not be understood as a civil war or the product of ethnic resentment. They believed that the war took place because ex-communist bureaucrats who had previously formed the Yugoslavia political, social, and economic elite during the socialist period wanted to keep their positions and thus used ethnicity and religion as tools to mobilize people into fighting. Explaining why Sarajevo became as embroiled as it did, they underlined the strategic importance of the capital city, noting that Sarajevo was the target of nationalistic aspirations for the creation of a "Greater Serbia." Sarajevo was also, locals argued, the actual seat of nationalist political leaders who enjoyed great power.

Some in Sarajevo compared their experience with the experiences of Bosnian rural areas and concluded that Sarajevo emerged as a relative "success story." They pointed to the fact that individuals and neighborhoods had been able to maintain close social relations across ethnic lines. They noted that war within the city was always on a small scale and that ordinary people worked together and did not turn against each other. However, they also noted that the proportion of the city's population that was Muslim grew from about 50 percent prior to the war to over 85 percent by the war's end.

Further, most people in the city said that they could not forget the war because they continued to experience its consequences. They said that the experience of the war had drawn attention to religious and national affiliations and differences that had seemed unimportant prior to the war. Mistrust among the three groups was being continued, they said, through a postwar educational system that was divided into three ethnic lines so that children of each group learned that their neighbors had been to blame for the war's occurrence.

Some also described a strong sense of victimhood among people who stayed in Sarajevo (and many were critical of this). For example, when they applied for a job after the war, people included in their curriculum vitae the fact that they had stayed in Sarajevo during the war and, because of this, felt that they deserved special consideration. The experience of victimhood also contributed, according to some people, to a sense of entitlement to state benefits and special opportunities for travel abroad.

Illustrating this, one person said: "We need to establish the dignity of victims. We do not need a Peace and Reconciliation Commission. My neighbors are not to blame! What we need is acknowledgment that the Serbian and Montenegrin Army was involved in the crimes and then we want justice. We could have a Victim Commission so that victims get justice."

Tuzla

The city of Tuzla in northeastern Bosnia had also been an ethnically mixed city for centuries, with Muslims, Croats, and Serbs living together. And during the war, when almost every other municipality saw ethnic strife and active ethnic cleansing, Tuzla remained ethnically mixed and united around a common identity. Tuzla was on the front lines of the war for nearly three years. Throughout these years, Serb, Muslim, and Croat citizens fought side by side in defense of the city, not for nationalistic loyalties or preeminence of one ethnic or religious group over others.

In the elections of 1990, Tuzla was the only major municipality that did not vote for a nationalist party. Instead, its citizens elected a Social Democrat as mayor, who remained the mayor throughout the war. In the postwar period, he became governor of the Canton of Tuzla, a larger administrative region. When he moved on to this new position, Social Democrats still controlled the administration of the city.

It was true that, as war had approached, tensions had mounted within the city. While all citizens were worried, the Serbs in particular felt a lot of pressure. As fighting began across the country, the war had quickly become defined as Serb against Muslim, and no one was certain what would happen in Tuzla with its Muslim majority. In this climate, some people left the city, and it was remembered that more of these were Serbs than members of any other group.

When the war began, the mayor and the municipality agreed that they would support the Bosnian Federation. The military units stationed in and around the city were offered a choice—they could support Bosnia or leave the city. On May 15, 1992, fighting occurred in and around Tuzla as military units decided which side to support. Many people recounted a "famous phone call" that they said the mayor made to his associate, the commander of the Serb units in Sarajevo. As a result of this call, they said, the commander agreed to leave the city and took up a position on the hills overlooking it. People were not actually sure that this phone call occurred, but it was "remembered" by many who claimed it had been an important factor in the city's ability to avoid ethnic fragmentation.

Responses to the War

As soon as the war started, the mayor of Tuzla established a war cabinet, consisting of the chief of police, the local army commander, and some of the civic department heads. This group met every morning to, as the mayor said, "prepare for the challenges for that day." They worked collectively to organize the defense of the city and the maintenance of the civil services at the same time. They agreed that the police department would remain a part of the civil service and not be assigned military functions or be used as an auxiliary force by the military. One result of this decision was that Tuzla did not experience much criminal activity during the war. Of the 600 workers in the municipality, only 60 left the city and their posts during the war. This commitment of the city workers to stay on their jobs was cited by many as inspiring to them to stay as well.

The chief of police was determined also to keep the police force multiethnic. He continued to hire new recruits during the conflict, making sure that they were drawn equally from all groups in proportion to their presence among the city's population and, over time, even increasing the representation of Croat and Serb officers on the force.

The army commanders who remained within Tuzla insisted that the units under their command should remain ethnically mixed. Individual soldiers who were unwilling to fight in a mixed army were also offered the chance to leave. One entirely Croat unit also chose to stay to defend the city and, in doing so, declared its loyalty to the Bosnian state.

Identity in Tuzla

The decision to stay in the city, even when many had opportunities to leave as the war intensified, was cited as a matter of identity and pride. When asked about why they stayed, many said, "I am from Tuzla, it was important to stay here" and "There are only two kinds of people from Tuzla, those who stayed and those who left." Notably, those who stayed did not consider those who left as Tuzlans any longer. Some said that being from Tuzla means that "you accept everybody." They contrasted their attitude from that of people from Sarajevo, where, they said, everyone knows what ethnicity everyone else is.

People in Tuzla expressed a feeling of smugness compared to other towns and cities. Tuzlans claimed that Sarajevans look down on them and call them "hicks" who are "not cosmopolitan." But they claimed that the "real reason" Sarajevans disdain Tuzlans is because "Sarajevo fell to pieces in the war and Tuzla did not."

Citing history as one explanation for their spirit of solidarity, which they claimed had "always" existed, Tuzlans said they have lived and worked side by side for centuries. Some claimed this stemmed from their history of 500 years earlier, when they were led by a Muslim, a Croat, and a Serb as they demanded concessions from their Turkish rulers. Others referred to the city's defiance of Austrian rule, and still others cited their pride in the city's engagement in Nazi resistance during World War II. Others claimed that solidarity grew out of labor organizations. Because it was an early industrial town in the Balkans, Tuzla was a hotbed of labor organizing during the nineteenth and twentieth centuries. Unions forged a strong sense of working-class solidarity across the ethnic groups and religions. Still others cited the strong socialist movement in Tuzla coupled with a relatively strong economy as factors that caused religion to fade as an influence on people's lives over many years.

During the war, people said that they found many ways to demonstrate and assert their solidarity—and singular Tuzlan identity. Oddly, because religion became such a significant divider during the war, it took on a new and heightened importance also in Tuzla. This was a surprise to people in Tuzla who had, as described earlier, placed socialism higher than religion in their history. The newfound emphasis on religion in Tuzla differed significantly from its emphasis in other cities, however.

During the war, celebrations of religious holidays became civil events, celebrated citywide. Celebrations of all sorts were important for morale, but also served to bring people together. In Tuzla, people became aware of their neighbors' different holy days and began to celebrate these with each other. Traditional foods were an especially important part of these celebrations. Everyone in a neighborhood would join together to cook the correct food for each holiday, even for others' religions.

Early in the war, the Bosnian Serb artillery fired a shell that destroyed a major Orthodox church in Tuzla. The mayor immediately called on all the workers who were involved in repairs in the city to move over to the church to rebuild it. These workers labored day and night, even under floodlights in full view of the gunners who had destroyed the church from a site on the hill. The mayor said that the church was important because "our citizens of the Orthodox faith need a place to worship. We must support them in their faith." Furthermore, he said that "this church belongs to all of the citizens of Tuzla and we cannot allow anyone from outside to destroy it."

The city also held secular events to bring people together. There were plays and concerts organized by the municipality as well as some that were organized spontaneously by citizens. At the suggestion of one person, and after consideration by the city leaders, the mayor formed an orchestra to "keep a smile on the face of the citizens." Musicians were commissioned to write new "patriotic" songs to assert the common identity of people of Tuzla as opposed to the messages of ethnic and religious divisions.

Late in the war, a sporting event was organized for the youth of the region. Young people from all over the area gathered in Tuzla to participate in athletic events. This gathering was attacked by artillery, and a shell exploded in the crowd, killing seventy young people and wounding many others.

Even with this tragedy, the mayor responded in a way that interpreted it as bolstering, rather than undermining, the togetherness that had characterized Tuzla's stance during the war. He immediately suggested that all the young people who had been killed should be buried side by side in a location provided by the city. The message would be one that demonstrated the unity of the city. A monument would be erected to all the youth of Tuzla. (This monument continues as a site of an annual memorial service for those who were killed.)

Most of the children's families agreed with this idea, but there was some reluctance on the part of some Muslim families who, it was reported, did not want their children buried alongside Christian children. The mayor inquired about who objected and met with these families to hear their concerns. It turned out that there were only a few Muslim parents who wanted their children to be buried according to their traditions. The mayor agreed that no one should be forced to bury their children in the common cemetery and that all traditions and concerns should be respected. Fifty families chose to bury their children in the common community memorial plot.

One family had a daughter who had been killed and another who had been injured. When the injured daughter came out of the hospital, she asked her parents where her sister had been buried and was told her sister was in the Muslim cemetery. The injured girl insisted that her sister must be reburied in the cemetery designated for victims of the tragedy alongside the others who had been killed. The parents finally agreed and the body of their daughter was moved.

Leadership

It is difficult to overemphasize the role the mayor played in maintaining the morale of the citizens of Tuzla. His indefatigable efforts even earned him a nomination for the Nobel Peace Prize when the war was over. He was described as "ubiquitous." He was "everywhere" and constantly exhorting people to stay cheerful and not to let the "enemy win."

The mayor, however, was not the only person in the city administration who was committed to the city's survival as an ethnically unified place. Civic and military leaders all played a visible role in keeping the city together and functioning.

In conversations about how Tuzla maintained its identity and unity throughout the war, one person said that he saw the mayor every day. When challenged about whether this was possible in a city of Tuzla's size, he then said, "Well, it seemed as if I saw him every day." Many people noted that they felt personally associated with their leaders and that they could easily discuss with them ideas or concerns. Elected leaders made it a point to walk around the city regularly, engaging people in conversations and asking for ideas and advice. They communicated city decisions and encouraged people to discuss them. In this rather large city, the fact that leaders chose to walk about and be accessible, and the symbolism of their being seen to be close to and listening to the people, played a significant role in maintaining a sense of awareness and inclusion among the citizens and in bolstering them in the face of adversity.

Case Writers' Analysis

The experiences of these two Bosnian cities are parallel in many ways. Both Sarajevo and Tuzla had long histories of good relations among ethnic and religious groups and of pride in this fact. Multiethnicity was an important aspect of the self-identity of each city and, both prior to and after the war, many citizens in both cities reaffirmed this. At the individual level, stories of heroism and caring for neighbors of a different ethnicity were common in Sarajevo. As individuals, many people did not succumb to the hate propaganda they were being fed. Still, many also speak about "those who fought against Sarajevo" as being "genetically" different—a reference to ethnicity as explanation for behavior. The constant bombardment of their city by Serb troops seemed to have undermined the commitment of many to respect Serbs.

It is true, however, that Tuzla also was surrounded by Serb troops stationed on the hills overlooking the city. And from time to time (but not continuously), these troops killed many and destroyed landmarks in the city.

But the experiences of these cities differed in two marked respects. The first explains in part the different reactions to the war and its ethnic-cleansing agenda. The leadership of Tuzla was a critical and central factor in support of the strategy of unity that the city pursued. The corresponding leadership in Sarajevo was similarly committed to making the city function under siege. Also physically located in Sarajevo, however, were the nationalist and military leaders who were committed to the agenda of ethnicity and ethnic cleansing. As Sarajevans noted, their city was the symbol for many of the capital of their ethnic group. As such, it was an important target and fighting arena.

Tuzla, by contrast, was guided by a leader not identified with nationalist politics but with the Social Democrats. Although he declared his and the city's loyalty to the Bosnian state early in the war, he did not do so with the fervor of ethnicity that this implied for other areas. His commitment was to maintain not only Tuzla, but also by extension Bosnia, as a multiethnic entity.

The second marked difference between the two cities reflects on their postwar experiences. In Sarajevo, the prevailing sense of victimhood differed starkly from the sense of efficacy and agency found in Tuzla. Even individuals in Sarajevo who maintained their personal commitment to multiethnicity, and did not support the ethnic agenda of the war, expressed their sense of victimhood. They felt they had been let down by the international community, which they judged as having "allowed" the war to happen. They felt victimized by the troops that had surrounded them. They felt victimized by the profiteers who had controlled the access to the tunnel. Many expressed their dismay at being powerless.

This difference is, in part, demonstrated in the two cities' responses to the physical destruction they experienced. In Tuzla, immediately after the shells destroyed the Orthodox cathedral, the mayor organized its rebuilding. In Sarajevo, years after the end of the war, many buildings remained as skeletons of their past and others still had the pockmarks of shells covering their surfaces. The extent of the destruction in Sarajevo was much greater than that in Tuzla, of course, but the differences in attitudes toward the destruction are still noteworthy. One community felt they could and should rebuild; the other felt they could not.

The stories people in each city told about the lead-up to war were also strikingly different. In Sarajevo, people described themselves as naive, believing that they would surely not engage in ethnic warfare and, at the same time, expecting that the international community would intervene to prevent war on their behalf. In Tuzla, people anticipated that the war would affect them and took steps to prepare their strategy for maintaining their way of life. This process of anticipation, analysis, and preparation was important in allowing the people of Tuzla to choose a position of nonengagement and in their continued pursuit of this position as the war ensued.

Note

1. Williams, "Sarajevo Threat Is Apparently Defused."

10

Colombia: A Story of Community Refusal

Colombia has experienced a repeating cycle of civil war and repression since at least 1948, the beginning of the notorious period known as La Violencia, during which partisan struggles led by Conservative and Liberal elites claimed the lives of over 200,000 people. La Violencia officially ended with a deal struck in 1958 in which the same partisan elites agreed to share power via alternating control of the "elected" government. This deal was a demonstration of the endemic problem of exclusion in Colombian politics and governance.

Background to the War

Colombia's wars have always been about real estate. La Violencia, often described as a feud between two political parties, was no different. It left many thousands of peasants landless as opportunists used the violence to expropriate lands from rural farmers and establish local fiefdoms. The Liberal-Conservative deal in 1958 meant that the elites stopped shooting each other, but the poor were still ruled by force.

This chapter is based on the original case study written in the field by Liam Mahony and Luis Enrique Eguren (see Appendix of Project Case Studies for full reference).

Emergence of Guerrilla Groups

In response, peasants in many cases banded together into armed self-defense militias to defend themselves and their land. The guerrilla group now known as the Revolutionary Armed Forces of Colombia (FARC) began during La Violencia as such a self-defense militia.

Many self-defense groups saw no reason to lay down their arms, and thus Colombia's modern guerrilla war was already under way when the end of La Violencia was declared. Over time, the FARC grew to the point of operating throughout the national territory. It embraced a communist ideology in the 1960s, and developed a strict military structure, a reputation for effective military tactics, and an elusive resilience. Meanwhile, many other guerrilla movements sprouted up, all within the same milieu of popular exclusion from control over politics, the economy, or land. Over time, many of these other groups engaged in negotiations with the government and demobilized. The FARC also entered into negotiations in the 1980s, but subsequently, demobilized FARC members were systematically exterminated by the thousands in an army-paramilitary campaign in the early 1990s, making the FARC deeply suspicious of any future negotiations.

The two primary remaining guerrilla organizations in Colombia are the FARC, with an estimated 15,000 combatants, and the Army of National Liberation (ELN), with an estimated 5,000 combatants (these figures vary widely). The largest Colombian guerrilla organizations have funded their operations primarily through what they call "taxation" of local economic elites.

Emergence of Paramilitaries

Prior to the mid-1990s, statistics showed that one of the major human rights abusers in Colombia was consistently the army. In the 1990s, under increasing international human rights pressure, Colombia needed to clean up its image and chose increasingly to "paramilitarize" its war. The result was a phenomenal decrease in abuses attributed to the army since 1997–1998, but a much larger increase in such abuses by paramilitaries.

When the case study was being written, an estimated 13,000 paramilitaries were represented by the United Self-Defense Forces of Colombia (AUC), an umbrella organization.[1] The AUC is universally acknowledged to have committed the majority of atrocities in Colombia. Carlos Castaño, the leader of the AUC until his death in 2004, and his colleagues were indicted numerous times, nationally and internationally, for murder and other human rights abuses as well as drug trafficking. Yet despite these indictments, Castaño was never arrested. He was killed in 2004 in what was claimed to be a mistaken shoot-out between his bodyguards and other fighters in the AUC.

The paramilitaries maintained close alliances with and received financial support from a range of Colombia's economic elites in order to facilitate the elites' economic strategies. This included involvement with the drug industry, the ranching business and the mining industry. They also had close connections nationally with financiers and speculators in numerous other businesses. These economic elites, in turn, were and are under pressure to promote international investment and resource extraction, which in turn, affected the paramilitary strategy.

Other Contextual Factors

Colombia's social landscape is also a crucial factor in understanding community attempts to create alternative spaces. The country is multiethnic, with a significant (about 20 percent) indigenous and Afro-Colombian population. It has been historically "regionalized" with minimal economic and social contact between different regions.

Colombia also has a history of nonviolent popular resistance, mass movements, union movements, and peasant mobilizations. The indigenous are proud of resistance efforts spanning 500 years, and the Afro-Colombian population has an impressive history of slave and freed-slave resistance movements. There is a long history of communal autonomy linked to resistance in these and other communities. This has emerged in opposition to conquest and because the abandonment of rural areas by the state created the necessity for self-sufficiency and self-defense. Communal autonomy has been recognized legally for both indigenous peoples and Afro-Colombians.

The Peace Community of San José de Apartadó

San José de Apartadó, a township founded in 1970, is located in the hills of Abibe. During the 1990s, San José comprised 3,000 people spread out among thirty-two villages. Some of these villages were as much as eight hours on foot from the town center of San José. Most of the inhabitants were white peasants who arrived in the middle of the twentieth century fleeing La Violencia in other regions.[2] The economy consisted of small-plot farming for subsistence and small-scale trade and some livestock ranching.

San José is separated from the city of Apartadó by a rugged uphill road. Although it takes only forty-five minutes by four-wheel drive to travel between the two communities, this distance creates a significant border and isolation. Until the early 1990s, the guerrillas had a regular presence in Apartadó, and in general in all the municipalities along the Pan-American Highway in the Banana Corridor.[3] Ranchers and banana plantation owners financed a long and intense struggle for control of the region between the guerrillas, the army, and paramilitaries. The conflict intensified in 1995 with the entry of the Self-Defense Militias Córdoba and Urabá (ACCU), the founding paramilitary organization of the national umbrella organization, the AUC. The situation was complicated by peace negotiations that led to the demobilization of the Popular Liberation Army (EPL), a guerrilla group, after which some of the EPL guerrillas were co-opted into the paramilitaries. There ensued a bloody war against other former guerrillas and all social organizations in the region. By the end of the 1990s, the army-paramilitary alliance gained control of the Pan-American Highway and the Banana Corridor.

But controlling the Pan-American Highway did not guarantee control of the entire region, because up in the hills and mountains (where San José was located), the guerrillas were still able to move about with relatively uninhibited access. Thus the military saw these hills as a strategic location to control, especially San José, because it is one of the key access points between the Banana Corridor and these mountains.

The combination in the 1990s of local military dynamics and the nationwide repressive campaign against the Patriotic Union made San José a frequent scene of combat and of attacks against the civilian population, eventually causing massive displacement.

In 1996, the Diocese of Apartadó, together with the Center for Research and Popular Education, the Inter-Congregational Commission for Justice and Peace (CIJP), and the Dutch nongovernmental organization (NGO) Pax Christi, proposed a new idea to the leaders of the community of San José: the creation of a "neutral zone" based on the principles of international humanitarian law. The plan was to achieve a higher level of respect for a civilian population committed to noncollaboration with all armed actors and to generate attention to this neutrality through formal declarations, external political support, and church-based and NGO-based development projects.

The discussions about this strategy lasted several months and were marked by the following dynamics:

1. Most of the discussions took place within the organizations that were proposing the strategy. The participation of the population was organized through a series of workshops, mostly attended by community leaders. The more general population was in some cases involved, but primarily only in the final ratification stage.

2. The process was influenced by a particular event outside the region that had national repercussion via the media. During that period, the communities of the Indigenous Organization of Antioquía publicly declared a strategy of "active neutrality." This organization had key leaders who were part of the government of Antioquía, led by Governor Álvaro Uribe Vélez (who later became president of Colombia), who co-opted this process, taking steps to institutionalize proposals for active neutrality and urging all communities to accept them. But Uribe applied this version of "neutrality" only to the communities' relationships with the guerrillas, thus distorting the concept and in turn leading many other communities to dismiss it, either because they disagreed with the concept or because they felt it would be impossible to sustain such a position of exclusion toward only one of the armed actors in regions where the guerrillas had significant influence.

3. Not all of the institutions involved in this process shared the same opinions about a "peace community." The Inter-Congregational Commission for Justice and Peace argued that to declare "neutrality" in such an unbalanced conflict, with profound social and territorial causes and impacts on civilians, signified the voluntary ceding of political space and liberty. The CIJP proposed that the communities declare themselves "communities in resistance."

Eventually a consensus was reached, and the population of San José de Apartadó formally decided to declare itself a "peace community." The Diocese of Apartadó consulted with the primary military actors in the zone, the FARC, and the paramilitaries, and these groups accepted in principle the existence of a peace community.

After a series of community consultations, the majority of the population approved the declaration of San José de Apartadó as a peace community.

Organizationally and socially, this began a complex process. Not all residents wanted to be a part of a peace community, yet the interactions of any resident with the armed actors in the region would affect the community's strategy. Further, the dispersion of tiny villages over great distances made unity and coherence difficult to sustain.

After considerable discussion, the peace community formally distinguished three groups within the population under its influence:

1. The civilian noncombatant population residing in the township who committed themselves to the Peace Community process,
2. The civilian population who would not participate in hostilities and committed themselves to the rules and statutes of the community, and
3. Other persons with a transitory presence in the community, who committed themselves to the statutes and rules and were thus covered by the statutes protecting the civil population.[4]

The third category demonstrated flexibility by allowing for temporary residency as long as the statutes and rules were accepted. Discriminating between members and nonmembers of the peace community was difficult in the distant rural areas where houses were quite isolated and community participation was minimal. However, no obvious tensions arose between the various member and nonmember groups in San José.

There were other tensions, however. For instance, community rules prohibited the selling of alcohol anywhere in the community for fear that it would attract combatants into the zone or provoke social disturbances. In a country with a considerable tradition of drinking, this rule led to many conflicts and debates, especially between the community leadership and the small merchants. But as the security situation worsened, the shared perception of risk helped to keep the rule in place, albeit with transgressions.

Protection Strategies

To generate public attention, San José made a formal declaration of its intent, announcing its explicit noncollaboration with all armed actors.

Noncollaboration

Noncollaboration required a set of rules to guide all interaction with armed actors and the internal behavior and functioning of the community. The community's declaration as a peace community laid out norms covering both areas. According to what were called "principles to orient the experience of civilian resistance," for instance, there were prohibitions against owning or carrying arms or munitions, participation in military operations, offering any logistical support or intelligence to any of the parties in conflict, and requesting support from armed groups.

Given the importance of intelligence-gathering to all armed groups, the prohibition against providing information was a crucial component of community neutrality. The prohibition against logistical support included a ban on selling even a soft drink to combatants who visited the community's small stores.

The Problem of "Visits" to the Community

One of the protection mechanisms that San José established was a system to control access to the community. This control was difficult to achieve in such an extensive, isolated, and mountainous territory. With the exception of the town center of San José, the rest of the villages in the township are located in the hills more than an hour away on foot, some more than a day's walk. The declaration of the peace community covered the whole township, especially as there was a desire to facilitate a return home of some of the population who had been displaced from outlying villages and were residing in the town center. But physical realities made control over access feasible only in the town center and in the closest village, La Union, while the rest of the area was constantly subject to the presence of combatants, depending on the ebb and flow of the conflict. The hills remained a passage for the guerillas and the scene of military operations.

The community was concerned about "unwanted" visitors—that is, unknown people in civilian dress who could enter the territory to gather intelligence for one of the armed parties. Because most of the villagers in the mountains knew each other well, and because such visitors tended to come in by the main road from Apartadó, the community decided to assume that all such visitors could be informants of the paramilitaries or the army. Sometimes, such visitors were asked to leave the town.

The Colombian Armed Forces

For the first five years of its existence as a peace community, San José tried to prohibit any entry into the town by the army, including even when the military wanted to serve as escort for government officials such as justice department personnel who visited the community. This demand was quite exasperating to the local army brigade, who argued that no part of the national territory could be off-limits to the armed forces. During this period, the community suffered paramilitary attacks and massacres that they believed to have been carried out in collusion with the local army brigade. It was clear that the army did not respond to protect the community even when there was substantial warning of an imminent attack.

The Fence

One development during this period was construction by the community of a small fence along the perimeter of the territory. It was entirely symbolic, yet it clearly delimited the territory of San José. Even after the army formally agreed not to be present in the community, as a form of pressure or provocation, soldiers would deliberately cross the fence and settle down for a rest, leaving only after the community had organized a formal delegation to protest their presence.

The Self-Displacement Ultimatum

Around 2002, facing continued precarious security conditions, the community tried a new approach to the army. This involved a compromise that allowed the army to pass through the community so long as it did not stay. The community acknowledged their location on a public thoroughfare and agreed to allow the army to pass through to the other side, even though the passage might be for the purpose of carrying out military operations.

This compromise was, however, accompanied by an ultimatum: In the face of repeated threats that the army intended to take up permanent residence in the town center of San José, the community declared in one of its assemblies that if this were to happen, the entire population of the town center would immediately displace itself to La Union indefinitely. The residents of La Union also declared that they would self-displace to the town center if the army installed itself in La Union. In an interview, one of the leaders stated: "If they want the town, they get the whole thing, but without us. We won't be victims of their combat on our own land when the others attack." This was not mere posturing. The entire community agreed on this stance, which guaranteed they would displace as threatened if necessary.

This ultimatum might seem counterintuitive, since the fundamental objective of the community's strategy was to prevent displacement. When asked about the risks of such a strategy, members of the directive council responded that to maintain their integrity in relation to the armed forces, they were prepared to sustain a long-term displacement if necessary and that they had made preparations for survival. They were concerned, however, about the possible destruction of their agricultural investments, such as mills, as well as that in the absence of witnesses, the army would plant evidence to later use against the community leadership (e.g., framing them with false arms caches.)

To minimize these risks, the community's strategy was to call on national and international institutions that were following the peace process, as an external delegation, to verify the conditions in which the community left its property so that whoever came in afterward would be legally responsible for that property. Community leaders could not predict what would happen next, and could not project long-term scenarios.

Presence of the Guerrillas, Proving Neutrality

The community equally opposed incursions by the guerrillas and knew it was crucial to demonstrate credibility nationally and internationally in this respect. From the start they requested a permanent presence of national and international institutions in their territory to monitor and thus demonstrate their commitment to neutrality. Peace Brigades International established a permanent presence in the community, and other groups such as the Fellowship of Reconciliation sustained temporary presences. Over time, the community also requested the permanent installation of a delegation of the state's Ombudsman's Office, but without success (the office argued that its presence in Apartadó was close enough to cover San José). Similarly, the community asked for a permanent delegate from the Presidential Office for Human Rights, which was also denied on grounds of resource limitations. In contrast, the community rejected the hypothetical idea of allowing the establishment of a police station in the town center, arguing that the police were armed and inherently had a military function due to the reality that they were being targeted by the guerrillas and would defend themselves against attack. Were this to happen, it would compromise the neutrality sought by the community.

Using the Inter-American Court

Based on a petition submitted by the Inter-Congregational Commission for Justice and Peace, the Inter-American Court of Human Rights in December 1997 authorized that the state should take measures for the protection of the San José community, including its inhabitants. In 2000 the court promulgated a new resolution demanding investigation of the attacks against the community and protection of the return of displaced residents. It also called on the state "to allow the petitioners to participate in the planning and implementation of measures and, in general, to keep them informed of progress made with respect to the measures ordered by the Inter-American Court of Human Rights." In this ruling the court recognized that the presence of armed forces in the community inherently posed a threat to civilians of retaliatory attacks from other armed actors. The ruling opened a space for the community to participate in discussions of the measures that would ensure their security. This process was later replicated in at least six other cases involving communities in Colombia.

Attacks Against the Community

The first armed incursion into San José occurred only five days after the community's peace declaration. Other serious attacks or incursions followed, most frequently by paramilitaries. In addition, in the initial period the FARC executed several people, including a highly respected historical leader of the community. It was thus clear from the beginning that the armed actors in the region were not happy with San José's peace strategy.

Since that time, there was an evolution in the paramilitary attacks against San José. In the beginning, each incursion left several community members murdered and this brought a loud reaction from the community and its national and international supporters. The community put great stock in its external accompaniment through the presence of international monitors as well as the support from other international allies for their capacity to generate prompt and effective political outcry. These outcries invariably placed responsibility on the nearby army brigade and its commanders, either as participants in the incursions or for lack of response to calls for help from the community. There were numerous testimonies from residents who recognized the soldiers involved in the "paramilitary" attacks, sometimes noting the insignia of the brigade on the clothing of these soldiers, or noting in one case that only twenty minutes after a paramilitary attack, the brigade arrived on the same road by which the paramilitaries had just exited. Each commander of the brigade found himself confronted by the peace community and its allies and was obliged to respond to accusations, including having to answer to the media.

After a certain point these paramilitary attacks, usually conducted at night, no longer left casualties among peace community members, but they continued to cause significant material damage. In one case, soldiers burned houses and threatened people by firing in the air. On another occasion, several small merchants operating in the community who were not formally members of the peace community were targeted and assassinated. In this incident, one of the peace community leaders tried to escape the attack by jumping off of a balcony, but one of the attackers, recognizing him, told him not to bother to run as this time he was not a target. This showed there was clear calculation of the targeting of victims based on some gruesome political cost-benefit analysis of the planners. After this attack, there were no more nighttime incursions.

The pressure did not stop, however, but was transferred to other venues such as the access road to San José. Paramilitary roadblocks, often located only a few hundred meters from a formal military roadblock, increased, limiting mobility and the transport of goods and causing economic hardship to the community. In addition, truckloads of goods headed from the community to market were robbed on the road. There came a point in 2002 when the paramilitaries were preventing all vehicular traffic in and out of the community, even assassinating the drivers of the buses or pickups. During this intense blockade, the only vehicles that were allowed to pass unmolested were the cars of Peace Brigades International and of the Diocese of Apartadó, again suggesting a careful political cost-benefit calculation. Responding to protests against this blockade, the army brigade produced aerial photographs purporting to show that the vehicles were carrying goods to the FARC. The community responded that these vehicles were carrying their own agricultural products and suggested that monitors or observers travel with the vehicles to prove it.

The economic blockade was devastating to San José, which had not been prepared for it. Facing a desperate lack of goods, the community assembly made a decision to march en masse to Apartadó to buy goods in a large group. But this proved unnecessary, as the diocese eventually broke the blockade through direct pressure and intervention. The bishop of Apartadó himself accompanied several truckloads of basic staples up to San José. After this, the blockade was less strictly sustained, and the community began to develop better strategies for self-sufficiency.

Specific Security Strategies

San José devised many defensive strategies to survive under threat, such as: always going out in groups to work the fields or to travel the roads, and reporting all exits and returns to the community, especially of members of the community council or other people facing particular risks. In addition, bells were installed in strategic locations as alarms to be sounded if incursions were suspected. The signal would call the entire population of a village to congregate in the plaza and confront the incursion with the moral force of numbers. If attackers asked to see the village's leaders, the collective response would be to refuse to identify them. But the alarm was not effective in some cases where the paramilitaries came in too quickly, commando-style, with lots of shooting. After suffering several assassinations and continuous death threats, the villagers used the alarm bell instead as a signal to flee the town center and hide in the hills until the attackers left.

External Support

External support was always a pillar of San José's peace strategy and proved to be crucial. The whole mystique of a "peace community" fit well into the Western imagination and gained broad international humanitarian and development support, such as from the Inter-American Court and Peace Brigades International as already mentioned, as well as from the international solidarity campaigns of "sister communities." In addition, lobbying efforts led to letters of support from members of the US Congress and other influential political figures, some of whom sent delegations to San José or visited the community themselves. One indication that such international presence was effective, in the case of Peace Brigades International, came when members of the army threatened San José that "those . . . people will not always be here."

Case Writers' Analysis

At the time of the case study, San José de Apartadó still occupied a strategic location, with a FARC presence higher up in the mountains. The army and the paramilitaries thus remained attentive, seeing it not as an enemy stronghold, but as a vital passageway they were unwilling to relinquish. The pressure focused on the highway leading to the town.

Since 1997 when San José declared itself a peace community, there were over sixty assassinations of residents. Over time, the constant intimidation prompted many families to leave the community, but at least half of its members remained. Clearly, this was a sign of both the strengths and weaknesses of the community's peace strategy. It should be remembered that Colombia has over 2 million displaced people and that the region in which San José is located was particularly targeted for displacement.

For the community project to stay alive despite such pressures suggests that the residents who stayed perceived a level of security in their united strategy and they trusted their capacity for economic self-sufficiency. They also had pride in their sense of ownership and connection to their land and in their commitment to active community participation.

Community participation in decisionmaking has flaws and weaknesses in any situation. However, San José sustained regular weekly or biweekly assemblies, and the community leadership displayed a high level of sensitivity to questions of accountability for its decisions without developing a tendency toward arrogance or self-enrichment. Rather, it persevered in the face of constant threats to personal security. For most, these factors apparently carried more weight than the sense of fear and stigmatization arising from the attacks and harassment.

Most important of all, perhaps, as community members themselves said, is the concept of dignity—their commitment to the right of any Colombian not to be expelled from his or her land, nor attacked for staying on it. This perception of collective dignity is undoubtedly a key factor that sustained the cohesion of the community of San José in the face of so many challenges.

Notes

1. The paramilitary universe is also full of factions, divisions, and power struggles, the complexities of which cannot be described here.

2. Ethnically in Colombia, *blanco* (white) signifies Latinos, or non-indigenous and non-Afro-Colombian people.

3. The guerrillas were mostly from the FARC, but also from the Popular Liberation Army (EPL) and the ELN.

4. *Declaration of the Peace Community of San José de Apartadó,* articles 2 and 3.

11

Mozambique: The Spirit of Mungoi

The Mungoi homestead near the town of Chidenguele has been described as an "island of peace" and as an "island of rest and commerce, an island of food and water" during a time of destruction and suffering of the war in Mozambique. In her book *A Different Kind of War Story,* Carolyn Nordstrom wrote: "The spirit Mungoi, angered by the war, not only protected the people who lived and traveled in his area from violence, he ensured that people kidnapped by Renamo were returned to their families. His area grew famous as a zone where people with violent intentions could not enter. It was an oasis in a sea of war."[1]

In the Mungoi homestead, people were able to sustain a primary school and agricultural crops at a time when this type of infrastructure was considered a strategic target by armed groups throughout the country. Also, anyone properly claiming to be from the people of Mungoi, or under the protection of Mungoi, either would not be kidnapped by Mozambican National Resistance (Renamo) forces or, when this fact was discovered after kidnapping, would be returned safely to the homestead. Anyone could approach Mungoi on behalf of a kidnapped relative and ask him to intercede with the warriors to have their relative escorted back safely to the homestead.

This chapter is based on the original case study written in the field by Tarah Farmen with Ezequiel Marcos and Egidio Vaz (see Appendix of Project Case Studies for full reference).

The case study explores how this community was able to function in the midst of war and to negotiate with both Renamo and the Liberation Front of Mozambique (Frelimo) to maintain their oasis of peace.

Background to the War

The Frelimo government came to power in 1975 after more than a decade of fighting against Portuguese colonial rule. It was considered a Marxist-Leninist government and received support from the Soviet bloc and China. For this reason, however, Rhodesia, South Africa, and the United States and North Atlantic Treaty Organization (NATO) allies considered it a threat to their political interests. When it came to power, Frelimo abolished the "traditional leadership," which it viewed as having collaborated with the colonial power. Pursuing its socialist strategy, it established communal villages and "dynamizing committees" and nationalized schools and hospitals. Religion was disallowed and targeted.

In addition, Frelimo encouraged the freedom movements in both Rhodesia and South Africa by allowing their rebel groups to operate from inside Mozambican borders. Rhodesia responded by initiating the formation of the Mozambican National Resistance (MNR), which later became Renamo, to fight, and unseat, the Frelimo government. Rhodesia maintained Renamo from 1977 onward until Rhodesia became the Independent Republic of Zimbabwe under Robert Mugabe in 1980. At this time, Zimbabwean support to Renamo ended. However, the South African apartheid government increased its funding, arms, and leadership support so that Renamo continued to grow.

In 1984, under pressure from both external and internal forces, Mozambique and South Africa signed the Nkomati Accord. Under this treaty, both countries agreed not to give material aid to opposition groups in the other's country. Mozambique complied by closing African National Congress (ANC) bases inside its borders, but South Africa unofficially continued to support Renamo until the war ended with a peace agreement, signed in Rome, in 1992.

Even with clandestine support from outside, Renamo troops had to gain provisions from the Mozambican population in order to survive. Thus, the war involved frequent assaults and raids on civilians that were often brutal. Armed groups also destroyed a great deal of infrastructure in order to undermine people's sense of government competence. Many families and villages were torn apart by the repeated incursions of military forces to recruit youth as fighters and to loot for supplies.

Chidenguele, Gaza Province

Gaza province provided the best transport corridor from the coast of Mozambique to the interior of the country. One person explained, "If I had to walk, this would be the natural valley I would take." In addition, the Portuguese had established ports and infrastructure along this corridor to facilitate trade with Rhodesia and South Africa. Some people felt that Gaza was, in part, protected from complete destruction by Renamo and Frelimo because the two armies saw this valley as a well-supplied path of retreat.

Nonetheless, Gaza province was deeply affected by violence throughout the war. Every person had been touched in some way. People reported that either they or a family member had been kidnapped, that a family member had been killed or never returned, that they had lost goods or property, or that they had had to move from their homesteads due to the war.

Both sides also recruited fighters—often forcefully—from among the people. Renamo regularly assigned its soldiers to operate in the area where they had been forcibly recruited "so they knew who the chief was and shared with commanders." Some noted that the result of this was that "brothers killed each other; communities killed each other." Similarly, Frelimo soldiers either "volunteered" or were recruited through conscription. Frelimo would approach the local leadership of villages, who would point out houses where young people lived in order to compile a recruitment list. Then Frelimo would send out a call to join the army. If the young men did not join willingly, they were rounded up and forced to do so. Sometimes, young boys were stopped on their way home from school and taken into the army. Overall, however, people noted that Renamo was more on the offensive in Gaza and Frelimo more on the defensive. This meant that people in Gaza ascribed their suffering during the war more to the former than to the latter.

The Mungoi homestead was located near Chidenguele, which is a town just off the national highway north of the provincial capital. The area is coastal, with some beaches on the Indian Ocean, some lagoons, and some hills. During the war, people often hid in the lagoons when armed groups approached. During the war, there was a Frelimo base in Chidenguele. The soldiers stationed there were "recruited" primarily from the area, so they knew who the traditional leaders were and who Mungoi was. When they described their area, most people in this region said that they were known for their hospitality.

The Mungoi Story

Prior to the war, the Mungoi family was not known as an especially strong family. During his lifetime, Mungoi was not recognized as a traditional "strongman" or a person people would go to with problems. However, his mother was known to be a powerful traditional healer, and he was seen to be a strong and able hunter. When Mungoi became prominent as a spirit protecting his people, many said he derived his power from his mother when he died.

Armando Mungoi, the younger son of Mungoi, had gone to Maputo for higher education and then worked in a factory in the city, but during the war he was called back to Chidenguele by the spirit of his father. He told the following story.

> My father's Spirit helped many people here. We witnessed many massacres. The Renamo soldiers came to our home soon before the massacre, and they looted the house. My father's Spirit began to think about all that had happened and got angry. I am sure my father's Spirit works. Its power comes from my father's mother. Twice, the Spirit complained to the rebels. The Spirit told the rebels that if they had to be at war, they should fight against the Frelimo soldiers because this is what war is all about but not attack and kill civilians.
>
> When the rebels attacked the Mungoi community, they kidnapped many people and took them to their stronghold. My father's Spirit appeared in one of the kidnapped women before the rebels and told them to release the kidnapped people. The rebels did not want to do what the Spirit was saying until the Spirit also appeared in one of the rebel's commanders known as "The Major."
>
> The rebels were impressed because their commander had changed his behavior showing he was possessed. Soon after the Spirit disappeared from the commander, they asked him where he had been. They told him what the Spirit had said and asked their

commander what to do. He then decided to release the kidnapped people back to the Mungoi area. The woman who had been possessed by the Spirit was asked by another woman whether they would find problems on their way back to the Mungoi community. The woman who had been possessed asked them to follow her and said, "I know the way and everything will be fine."

When they arrived back to the Mungoi homestead, the medium exorcised so that the Spirit could appear. Then the Spirit said to the rebel commander, "You wanted to burn my home and all my belongings and my children. Here you are and I would be happy to see that happen now as you promised. I tell you I will not burn because I died and I cannot die twice, and also I command you to destroy my tomb." The commander looked down at the Spirit and said, "I would like to have a way to know who your people are who are at the bases so that anytime I can release them."

"People of Mungoi" as an Identity

The spirit established a system for people to identify themselves as Mungoi's people. To prove that you were one of Mungoi's people, you needed to recite the genealogy of the spirit going back about three generations on both the mother's and father's sides. A traditional leader said: "Protection was for the people, for the community. The rebels would come but were unable to take people provided they were able to say the family tree. It was for anyone in the area." If you were not of the Mungoi family, but asked for protection from the spirit, you would be told the genealogy, which could be used to verify whether someone claiming to be one of Mungoi's people was "telling the truth."

Negotiating with Armed Groups

The son, Armando, described his own interactions with armed commanders in both armies:

> In the wartime, people would come to our homestead and report the rebels had kidnapped people. I would walk towards the rebels to rescue the people, or if they were too far away, I would take a car and tie a white flag to it. If they saw me they would stop and the commander would come to me and ask, "What wrong have we done?" Then I would respond by saying I just need my people back,

> my father's Spirit has sent me here. Sometimes the people had been looted or had their money taken by the rebels, and then they would return back to the Mungoi community.
>
> We had a lot of people who were released from the strongholds and sent to the Mungoi area. When the Mozambique government learned of this, my father's Spirit asked the local leadership to call the Governor to participate in a big party, because the Mungoi wanted to communicate that the Spirit was getting ready to go to war. This happened and it is from this time that Frelimo officially was made aware that the Mungoi Spirit was fighting to protect the population.

In a separate conversation, the president of Chidenguele (a traditional leadership position) recalled that when the spirit Mungoi decided to take an active role against the armed combatants, he called the local traditional authorities to the Mungoi homestead: "The Spirit saw it was not possible to fight alone. He needed to let the local authorities and the local administrator know. And the Spirit invited them to his home. I was there. The Spirit said, 'I want to begin fighting. They (Renamo) are saying they are not against community living, but now we realize they are burning shops, schools and people's properties. So I am telling you I sent word to the Renamo soldiers. I told them they are not allowed to take civilians especially from this area. I told them, don't come to Chidenguele.'"

Confronting Armed Groups

People also reported that the spirit Mungoi used various supernatural means against the soldiers. When Renamo tried to steal goods from the Mungoi homestead, the spirit inflicted them with blindness and caused them to lose their way. Then the spirit caused them to fall asleep and allowed Frelimo soldiers to find them and attack them. The spirit later explained to Frelimo soldiers that if they tried to steal from the Mungoi family, the same would happen to them. A number of people also told stories of the spirit setting bees against Renamo soldiers who stole from or kidnapped the people of Mungoi. A few people reported the use of darkness, lights, and mysterious sounds. Sometimes the spirit appeared "in a white suit and very tall so that nobody could see his head." Other times, he was described as appearing with a top hat or holding an old hunting rifle.

One woman who had been kidnapped and held in a Renamo stronghold told the following: "There was a day he appeared in the rebel's stronghold and the rebels tried to shoot him on several occasions and he made water come out of the guns, and later he brought darkness in the area so that we could not see each other. The rebels handed over all their weapons and stopped fighting. Another time they tried to kill civilians using a long knife and the Spirit caused their hands to dry up. Mungoi was such a good guy. When people were released, they were taken by the Spirit to his home. He would care for those whose homes were far from the Mungoi area, find clothing and heal them from diseases they had and then would request his own Spirit to accompany them back to their original areas."

Another woman who had also been kidnapped and held in a Renamo stronghold for over a year recounted that there were three ways the spirit would appear to the soldiers: by possessing a civilian woman who had been kidnapped, either on the way to or after arriving in the stronghold; by possessing a soldier on the way to the stronghold; or, if both of these failed to be convincing, by possessing one of the rebel leaders, even a commander.

Yet another woman who had been kidnapped and held for four months told the following of her experience: "One day a rebel commander requested everyone to come together and said 'You are free to go home.' But this happened because the Mungoi Spirit appeared in one of the rebel commanders. There were those which were considered the Mungoi's but this time, he released everyone. I returned to the Mungoi community. We thanked him not because we were compelled to do so. He said to us that we suffered a lot and hence he did not want us to pay him for the service done."

Hospitality and Maintenance of Agriculture

As the war continued and soldiers became increasingly responsible for obtaining their own supplies, it became more important to "prove" you were protected by Mungoi. A woman who had been kidnapped said determination of who was "protected" was made after kidnapping and before arriving at a stronghold. She said the Renamo soldiers would ask, "Who are the guys coming from the Spirit's place?" and these people would be taken back to the Mungoi homestead.

The fact that kidnapped people were escorted back home was emphasized by many. Despite the ongoing war and destruction of infrastructure, the Mungoi homestead was able both to provide for the growing number of people staying there and to provide food and supplies to the soldiers who escorted people back after kidnapping. People said that because they were not under immediate threat of attack, they were able to continue farming. The processes that protected them also permitted, and relied on, the maintenance of normal production. Life was still not easy, though, and most people in the area depended not only on their farms but also on supplies such as rice and clothing from larger towns.

Providing hospitality strained community resources, but people seemed never to waiver in seeing this as central to their identity and survival strategy. They said, "Whenever people were escorted back by Renamo, the Mungoi homestead which was not a big community had to prepare food. Sometimes Renamo would have to bring back the food they stole, and when they brought it back, the Mungoi people would let them eat there. Sometimes as soldiers would prepare to go back to their stronghold, Mungoi would give them one whole chicken for fifteen to thirty guys. He would tell them to take this as your food. And he would give them one bottle of wine. They would get completely drunk and by that single chicken, they were well fed."

Clearly, Renamo soldiers were often sent on missions to procure supplies for their bases. When they did this, they not only needed to obtain food and goods, but also needed help with carrying the food and goods back to their strongholds. Therefore, the soldiers continued to raid and kidnap people from the Mungoi area even though they knew they were required by the ancestral spirit to escort the kidnapped people back home. They also knew that when they brought the people back, they would again be fed, as well as protected from attacks by Frelimo for a while, and that they would be given food for their journey back to their stronghold.

The rules set out by the spirit Mungoi were clear and if any armed group broke these rules, they knew they would be punished. If they followed his rules, his system allowed them to be resupplied.

Security

Many people accepted the protection of the spirit Mungoi. A number of people said that they believed that even after one left the area of

Chidenguele, Mungoi's power to protect continued. In this, belief about the power of the spirit Mungoi differed from the traditional view that the power of a chief or strongman derived from his ancestors and was rooted in the land and could not be transferred to another place.

The community of Mungoi developed other strategies for security even as they relied on their ancestral spirit. Some also described ways in which they hid in the bush or the lagoons when they were warned that soldiers were approaching the area. When they were asked why they hid even though they believed they were protected by Mungoi's spirit, one said to the case writer, "Oh my child, you have but one life to live and you just never know." Others suggested that the spirit was not always present. They noted that, when people did not receive protection, "perhaps the Spirit was somewhere else that day." Many people in the Gaza region spoke of being helped by the spirit Mungoi or told of others being helped by him. They said that, when helped, people thanked the spirit and the Mungoi family out of gratitude (to "thank" the spirit meant to offer gifts of some kind).

Anyone could seek help from the spirit Mungoi, even outsiders. For example, a number of people said that if you had a relative kidnapped, you could go to the Mungoi homestead and tell the spirit the name of your relative. The spirit would write down the name and, immediately, your relative would be released and the commanders would instruct their soldiers to escort this relative home.

You also did not need to be native Mozambican to ask for assistance. There was an Indian shopkeeper who came to the Mungoi homestead and asked for help because his wife had been kidnapped. According to the story, she was returned safely to him and he was so thankful that he stayed at the homestead and built a roundhouse for the spirit.

Mungoi and Frelimo

Fewer people told stories of Mungoi's interventions with Frelimo soldiers. One man noted that "Mungoi could manage to have the army and rebels meet without fighting." He continued: "Mungoi wears a white suit and appears in a woman. One day, the Spirit arrested many rebels and asked them to put all weapons aside and enter his house. He then asked somebody to call the Frelimo soldiers and when they arrived, they opened fire for quite a long period, but surprisingly through the powers of Mungoi, no one was injured because the Spirit could hold a cow's tail and wave it [to make others] bulletproof."

Because Renamo soldiers so often kidnapped people from the Mungoi homestead and then returned them, it was natural that Frelimo would be suspicious of these frequent comings and goings of its enemy to the Mungoi homestead. A former Frelimo soldier noted that he and his comrades did have some suspicions that the spirit Mungoi was collaborating with Renamo, but were reassured by the fact that when the spirit brought kidnapped people back, someone would come to the Frelimo stronghold and tell them the rebels were nearby. When the Frelimo soldiers wanted to meet with the spirit to seek protection for themselves or their relatives, they had the choice of either leaving their weapons and going to the Mungoi homestead or keeping their weapons and meeting with the spirit outside the boundaries of the homestead. This same soldier said that he and his comrades preferred to keep their weapons and not enter the homestead, because they "respected the Spirit's power." Another Frelimo soldier indicated that the spirit sometimes helped them by giving them information such as "go this way and you will see the paths the rebels use and their weapons will not work." But others explained that this only occurred when the rebels had broken the "agreement" with Mungoi by kidnapping or stealing from the homestead.

One former Frelimo soldier with the surname Mungoi told the case writers, "My father used to leave his ID on the table so Renamo soldiers who came would see he was Mungoi. We had cars and goods but they never bothered anything. He never locked the doors so that they would not blow the doors open." He also had a female relative abducted by Renamo. When it was learned that she was Mungoi, she was escorted home unharmed. This former soldier also told us that people still respected the power of Mungoi. Although he was not at the homestead during the war, he said that people still sometimes thanked him for helping their families during the war. He said that one time it even helped him get out of a speeding ticket!

One woman reported that in 1994, "many people and local leadership and the government were mobilized to go to Mungoi and express gratitude for the good work he did in conflict prevention and resolution."

Challenges to the Spirit

Some people chose not to seek the protection of Mungoi. These included individuals or families who moved to other towns or cities, people who chose to believe in God's protection instead of that of Mungoi, and some people who simply chose not to believe.

It was difficult to continue living in the villages, as people were under constant threat of a surprise attack from Renamo. Only those who had the means to leave could do so, and often made this move after a close family member was killed. But even that was a dangerous choice, because the convoys in which they traveled were also targets of frequent attacks. And even cities were under threat. Some said that around Maputo, shooting could be heard in the suburbs.

One who chose God over Mungoi said: "God was our protector. We abandoned the Spirit Mungoi. God knew we would not have time to plow the land so there was no rain. So you may ask how we survived in the bush. The answer is that we survived mostly because we believed God was protecting us." Another said: "People went to church every Sunday. The church did not encourage people to get help from the spirits. They said for us to use our own weapons, the Bible and prayer." Others gave credit to both the spirit Mungoi and the church. "Peace came about because of the Spirit and because of prayers and fasts."

Finally, some said they did not believe in or seek protection from the spirit Mungoi because people were required to give goods and service in thanks for the protection and safe return of loved ones.

Case Writers' Analysis

One way to understand the success of invoking the spirit Mungoi is as a strategy that satisfied everyone's needs while allowing the community to opt out of war. When people were kidnapped, soldiers who returned them would be given food to take back to their strongholds. The "rules" were well established and, when followed, worked to everyone's advantage.

But there was a powerful contrast between what occurred in this community compared to the experiences of other communities and in the scope of who this strategy was able to affect. There were political reasons for people in Gaza who wanted to adhere to traditional practices to oppose Frelimo. Traditional leaders were banned first by the Portuguese and then by Frelimo. In the absence of government, local leadership and spiritual leadership took action to protect the community from violence. Mungoi's powers, in contrast to the effects of strategies pursued by other communities, expanded to protect beyond the traditional limits of linkage to land and place. It went beyond a local or narrow definition of identity. Anyone was welcome to Mungoi's protection, and many were indeed protected.

Although the nature of the war varied across Mozambique, it can be said that the fighting was experienced community by community. This is what makes it remarkable that the Mungoi community was able to negotiate with both Renamo and Frelimo.

At a time when some of the external funding for conflict prevention was targeted at building civil society and educating youth and finding jobs for young men, it is significant that the Mungoi people were not persuaded to adopt these approaches. Instead, the credibility of elders and traditional leaders enabled them to call upon a set of shared beliefs to help them function during a time of war.

Meeting the Spirit: Report of a Case-Study Writer

> When we met with Armando Mungoi, he told us that it would be best for us to meet directly with the Mungoi Spirit. So, we all piled into a truck to travel to the Mungoi homestead, and were joined by an older woman. As we had not had lunch or refreshment, I opened a water bottle to pass around the truck which she eagerly shared with us. The Mungoi family homestead was about a twenty-minute drive over established dirt roads from the center of Chidenguele. We passed a group of buildings that were pointed out to us as the school that had remained open during the war. Along the way, we asked about the proper way to greet the Spirit when we were to meet him.
>
> When we arrived, it appeared the family was preparing a meal. The women greeted the old woman who came with us with "jokes" about this not being the correct day or time for the Spirit to work. I wanted to let them know that we were in no hurry and could come again another day. However, we had not been greeted yet so we sat still under a tree and could not speak or make eye contact. Eventually, we were greeted and invited to take off our shoes and enter Mungoi's house. This roundhouse was quite large compared to others and was whitewashed inside.

The woman who had ridden with us turned out to be the medium for the Spirit. She went through the ritual to call the Spirit upon her. A small boy, who was Mungoi's namesake, imitated her movements as the Spirit possessed her. During the ritual, Mungoi's daughter and son assisted by dressing the medium in a white cloth and a man's black top hat. The medium's voice changed.

The Mungoi Spirit circled around us twice and then sat on a large chair facing us with his son on his right and his daughter on his left. A small table was placed between us with a vase of silk flowers upon it. The family members greeted the Mungoi Spirit individually with brisk rhythmic hand claps and they announced our presence and the purpose of our visit. The Spirit greeted us in the traditional way and it was then our turn to explain our purpose in meeting him.

Mungoi told the same story as his son, Armando, adding two additions. He said that one day he had gone hunting and realized upon his return that the rebels had come, looted everything and kidnapped his granddaughter. His mother's spirit was very angry and appeared to him. The Spirit also told us his full name and matrilineal lineage two generations back just as people were told to do during the war time in order to prove they were one of his people. He told us it was good that we came to speak with him first because, as we went forward with our interviews, we could ask other people to recite this genealogy and in this way, we would know who was telling the truth. Mungoi also said he was present and persuasive when the Peace Accord negotiations for ending the war were held in Rome.

The son told us that many people had stayed at the homestead during the war. Some were there waiting for relatives to be returned. Some stayed when they were escorted back by soldiers and waited for other family members to come find them. And others stayed for protection.

When our time with the Spirit was over, we thanked Mungoi and the family for their time. We had been told that it would be appropriate to present Mungoi with gifts which we did and these were recognized as familiar gifts and accepted. The medium "exorcised" again and then we gave her a ride back to Chidenguele as she had more work to do elsewhere that night.

Note

1. Nordstrom, *A Different Kind of War Story*, p. 148.

12

Rwanda: Muslims Reject Genocide

In Philip Gourevitch's well-known book on the genocide in Rwanda, *We Wish to Inform You That Tomorrow We Will Be Killed with Our Families,* he wrote that the Muslim community "apparently behaved quite well, and as a group, was not active in the genocide, even seeking to save Tutsi Muslims."[1] This case study explores the accuracy of this perception.

Background to the War

Islam was introduced into Rwanda through trade in the late nineteenth century. Muslims who immigrated were Arab and Indian traders and their assistants from Tanzania, and scholars and religious leaders who were later brought in by Rwandan Muslims to educate and lead the growing Muslim population. As the community became established, they attracted converts and many Muslim men married Rwandan women. By the 1990s, the Muslim community constituted approximately 10 percent of Rwanda's population and were no longer ethnically distinct. As with other religious faiths in Rwanda, the Muslim community included both ethnic Hutus and ethnic Tutsis.

This chapter is based on the original case study written in the field by Kristen Doughty and David Moussa Ntambara (see Appendix of Project Case Studies for full reference).

Historically, the relationship between Muslims and those in power—traditional leaders, the colonial administrations, and then the governments of the first and second republic after independence—was tense. From the beginning, Rwandan traditional leaders resisted the Muslim traders' penetration in Rwanda, fearing they would expand the slave trade from Tanzania. In addition, many European missionaries who came to Rwanda to prepare the ground for colonization saw Islam as a threat. Because the Christian church leadership was closely linked to the colonial leaders, an anti-Muslim sentiment became codified in discriminatory official policies. The authorities' antagonism toward and marginalization of Muslims continued under the various postindependence regimes. The marginalization of Muslims took place in three main ways: through separate education, restrictive settlement patterns, and lack of access to participation in governance.

During colonial times, primary and secondary education were delivered through Christian schools. Muslims had the opportunity to attend these schools but if they did, most faced efforts on the part of their teachers to convert them. Those who did not convert were frequently unable to continue school beyond the elementary level.

Many Muslim parents, fearing conversion attempts, did not send their children to school at all. Others sent their children to quranic schools. Because they did not have access to the Christian education that provided educational and networking opportunities, Muslims remained economically and politically marginalized, involved in petty trade and jobs that had little influence on the colonial or indigenous administrations.

Another factor of colonial administration, in agreement with the indigenous administration, was the establishment of a policy that Muslims must live in defined settlement areas. A decree passed in 1925 specified that no one in a settlement area could own land; residents were allotted land use for periods of only twenty years. The decree also specified that there could be no farming or animal raising in settlements; that settlement inhabitants were required to have a residence permit; that any Muslim going into any other Rwandan community needed a permit; and that any Rwandan citizen from outside a settlement was required to have a permit to enter.

Muslims in settlements had a separate and parallel governance system with their own appointed leaders who reported to the colonial administration. They also had their own courts. At the same time,

Muslims were not obligated by the colonial administration to participate in forced labor, a common practice in the rest of Rwanda prior to independence. Exemption from forced labor and the right to self-defined leadership both provided a level of comparative privilege to Muslims and also ensured their marginalization within Rwandan politics and society.

These patterns continued after independence. By 1994, most Muslims still lived together in groups and former settlement areas were still predominantly Muslim. Even in rural areas that had not traditionally been settlements and where there were fewer Muslims, they still lived in groups rather than scattered throughout the hillsides.

Muslim-Tutsi Relations

Historically, Muslims had an informal allegiance with the Tutsi elite. In many areas of Rwanda, they developed social and business relationships with the ruling Tutsi aristocracy as their dressmakers, drivers, mechanics, and the like. These relationships extended to sharing food and sports, but did not translate into political favors (as Muslims did not participate in government) or social favors (as Muslims still faced discrimination in schools). With the start of multiparty politics in the late 1950s, both Muslim Hutus and Tutsis sided with the party that claimed independence from Belgium, which was affiliated with the king and the Tutsi aristocracy. This relationship, however, was not a significant factor in the Muslims' choice to exempt themselves from participation in the genocide.

The Genocide

In April 1994, a plane carrying the presidents of Rwanda and Burundi was shot down above the airport in Kigali. The plane crash, blamed by Hutus on Tutsi rebels, triggered what appeared to be a coordinated attempt by Hutu extremists to eliminate the Tutsi population. Within hours, a campaign of violence spread from the capital throughout the country.

Much of the violence was neighbor-on-neighbor. Many of the people who killed their fellow Rwandans, often with machetes, were not strangers but had grown up together, gone to the same churches and schools, shared the same language, and were often related through intermarriage. Many Hutus who did not themselves kill colluded in the murders by revealing people's hiding places to the militias.

The genocide was not a spontaneous eruption of hatred and killing. While the violence occurred largely at the civilian level in the communities, many observers note that the genocide was fundamentally a "crime of the state." It was masterminded and organized by high-level politicians, military officials, and businessmen who set the stage through disseminating strategic inflammatory Hutu-power and anti-Tutsi propaganda through the schools and media, and in their political rhetoric. The initial violence was carried out by highly organized state armies and coordinated Interahamwe militias comprising groups of armed youth who killed and terrorized. Civilians became involved often with coercion from soldiers and police officers who forced them to "kill or be killed." In addition, community members were given incentives, including food, money, or being told that they could "inherit" the land of the Tutsis if they killed them. The radio broadcast Hutu-power propaganda, and travel restrictions prevented people from moving safely around the country to assess the situation for themselves. Mayors and administrators were often under the influence of political and army leaders. The groups of people who were doing the killing controlled what was happening in many communities.

Throughout the genocide, there was virtually no security across the country and many people felt that it was impossible not to get involved. People suspected of protecting others were often sought out and killed by their own communities. Nonetheless, there are many stories of individual Rwandans who took heroic steps not only in order to avoid participating in the killings but also in an effort to protect others. But these stories represent isolated actions of individuals that did not translate into group actions.

Muslim Community Actions During the Genocide

Both Muslims and non-Muslims in Rwanda recognize that the vast majority of the Muslim community did not participate in the genocide but rather acted positively, with many Hutu Muslims protecting Tutsi Muslims and non-Muslims. There were examples of both passive resistance in which people did not participate, and active resistance in which people took risks to protect others, sometimes losing their own lives in the process. This was true across the country, in both rural and urban Muslim communities.

Four factors have been repeatedly cited as "proof" of Muslim actions nationwide:

1. No Muslim religious leaders were subsequently charged or arrested for participating in the genocide.
2. No one who sought refuge at mosques was killed with the collusion of the Muslim leadership, in contrast to instances where people sought refuge in churches and state offices only to be killed on the order of, or with the cooperation of, religious or state leaders. When people died at mosques, they were killed despite the active resistance of Muslims and non-Muslims protecting them there.
3. After the genocide, it became clear that a disproportionate number of survivors, both Muslim and non-Muslim, had been protected by Muslims.
4. Very few Muslims were later imprisoned as a result of genocide investigations.

Direct Actions to Save Others

One Muslim said, "You will find very few Muslims who did not hide others." Many hid both Muslims and non-Muslims who were being hunted. When militias came to kill people, rather than turning the wanted people in, Muslims protected them, often sending the sought-after person over their back fence to another Muslim person's home for protection. As one person said, "Whoever managed to arrive in our quarter was hidden and protected and survived." Muslims described hiding people in their ceiling rafters and giving women veils and scarves to disguise themselves.

They took the role of helping rather than, themselves, fleeing. Someone said, "When people were massively running away before the advancement of armed groups, Muslims continued to hide their wanted colleagues." People who could do so went out to buy food, drink, and medicine and bring these items back to the people being hidden.

When anyone in the Muslim community seemed to be leaning toward violence, others tried to correct and shape that person's behavior. For example, when one community member encouraged his colleagues to get involved in the escalating violence, others asked him, "Do you really want to do that? If so, we would have to start with your wife since she is a Tutsi." He apparently did not try to provoke anyone after that.

Confrontation

In some instances, Muslims directly engaged with militia members. In one town, they attacked and destroyed the residence of an Interahamwe member in order to compel him to stop. Others took great risks in confronting and talking with those who were killing, trying to get them to stop. Some Muslims offered to pay militias not to kill. Others said, "You will have to kill me first." When the mayor of one commune urged active involvement in the genocide, the Muslim community organized themselves and went to the office of the district officer, asking for advice on what they should do. He told them they should take the refugees to the district office. But people knew that all across Rwanda, people were being killed at district offices in this way. So, one Muslim member of this commune explained, "We refused to hand people over. I told him myself, 'We want to rescue these people. If you want to take their cows, go ahead, but let us protect the people.'"

Direct confrontations did not always succeed. In one case, killing broke out on one side of a lake and Muslims who lived on the other side used their canoes to save many Tutsis who had been thrown into the water to drown. The news circulated in the area and most Tutsis from neighboring communities fled to this area. When they saw that the Muslims were receptive, they hid in the mosque. As the only safe haven for the hunted Tutsis and moderate Hutus in the area, the mosque became crowded by asylum-seekers.

When the Interahamwe came to kill people in this village, the leaders of the mosque refused to hand them over. They asked, "Why should a Tutsi die?" Resistance was stiff. The Interahamwe killed the Muslim leader on the first day. The Muslims and refugees at the mosque continued to fight with the Interahamwe for three days using traditional weapons, such as bows and arrows and rocks. On the fourth day, police reinforcements armed with guns arrived and defeated the group at the mosque. Many people died in the confrontation, including the leaders of the resistance. Survivors helped the wounded and escorted surviving refugees to territory controlled by the Tutsi-led army.

When the genocide broke out in Kigali, again wanted Muslims and non-Muslims gathered in a mosque compound under the Muslim leadership. When the Interahamwe militia tried to take the Tutsis, everyone there told them, "There is no Hutu, no Tutsi. We are all simply human beings." The leadership refused to give up the Tutsis and placed guards around the mosque. The group resisted the Interahamwe for three days. Meanwhile, Tutsis who were able to escape from other areas, including from churches, also fled to this mosque. The presidential guards then came in and demanded that the Hutus separate themselves from the Tutsis. Again, everyone refused. They told the militia, "We know that you came here to kill. If that is what you want, please kill all of us but not a section of this community." This "negotiating" did not work and the presidential guards shot into the group. Many were killed; others scattered and were killed as they fled.

Nonparticipation and Trickery

Other strategies were also used. Some Muslims pretended they were going along with the genocide in order to defer suspicion and avoid attack even while protecting people. Some Muslims chopped down banana trees and organized burials for the trunks in order to pretend they were burying people they had killed. Some infiltrated and spied on the militias in order to inform Tutsis about the times of killers' attacks.

In the former settlement areas, people did not hide in mosques but in Muslims' houses, where they were protected by being moved from house to house. In the areas of Muslim expansion where Muslims were intermingled with non-Muslims, people gathered in mosques because they were afraid their neighbors would turn them in. In general, the former settlement areas were more passive in their nonparticipation in the genocide; in areas of expansion, Muslims were more active in their resistance.

Faith and the Reinforcement of Identity

Muslims named their Islamic faith as the primary explanation for their nonparticipation in the genocide. They cited three key teachings of the Quran: that the Quran teaches nonviolence, with the killing of one person being a sin equivalent to killing all of humanity; that it teaches not to differentiate based on labels but rather that all people are equal; and that it teaches to protect the weak and assist people who are discriminated against.

People also said that the fact that they pray together five times a day reinforced their faith and their sense of involvement with each other. They noted that it is difficult to fathom killing someone with whom you kneel several times a day to pray. Practices such a paying religious taxes as a means of sharing with the community and sharing food were named as important aspects of social organization and cohesion that were central to the Muslim doctrine.

The genocide began just a few weeks after Ramadan, the holiest of Muslim periods, which involves inner reflection, devotion to God, and self-control. During Ramadan, Muslims fast during the day as a means of purification and self-discipline and as a means of identifying with those in need and developing sympathy for the less fortunate. In addition, Ramadan emphasizes the strength of the community, and Muslim ideals of sharing with others are amplified as people eat the break-fast meal together after sundown and share food with each other. Particularly during this period, the solidarity within the Muslim community as they performed the rituals together was strong. When the genocide began just a few weeks later, the strong cohesiveness within the Muslim community and the ideals of the Quran were still very present in people's minds.

One non-Muslim said, "Muslims are really living their religion." People noted that Muslims were "not Muslim in name only." Having been marginalized and discriminated against, Muslims took their religion seriously and affirmed their coherence and identification with their fellow Muslims. The identity of being a Muslim superseded other possible identities; being a Muslim was more important to almost all Muslims than their ethnic identity as either Hutu or Tutsi.

Leadership and Identity

As noted, no Muslim religious leaders were implicated in the genocide. Many in fact are reported to have taken concrete actions to shape the community's responses against the genocide. Prior to the genocide, both religious leaders and Muslim teachers recognized the polarizing political situation with the increase of propaganda and the justification of violence in political rhetoric. They thus anticipated the violence. As a result, they took deliberate and specific actions to emphasize certain community norms counter to the national situation.

They sensitized the population to reject the hate propaganda. They cited the teachings of the Quran and instructed people not to participate in violence when it came. Teachers worked actively with their students in Muslim schools, reminding them that all people are equal, ethnicity should not be divisive, and people should not kill but should try to rescue victims. As one person involved in this campaign said, "The Prophet tells us that a time of temptation will come, and we considered this a time of temptation."

The Muslim leadership also spoke out publicly in ways that could reach non-Muslims as well as Muslims. This was clearly quite risky as it could call attention to the resistance of the Muslim community. In 1993, as the situation in the country was becoming increasingly volatile and violent, the Muslim leadership issued a "pastoral letter," posted in mosques around the country, calling upon Muslims to avoid becoming involved in any political parties that involved ideologies or actions counter to the teachings of the Quran.

The leadership also issued announcements and submitted them to government-owned radio in which they told Muslims that hard times were coming and appealing to them to adopt positive values and not implicate themselves in the coming events. While some of these announcements were censored, several were broadcast. It is not clear exactly why some of these messages were allowed, but people did notice that messages sent out over the radio during the genocide were contradictory at times. On some occasions the radio announced declarations against the genocide, but most believed that these were intended to create a false sense of security to lure Tutsis out of hiding and to give the international community the impression that things were under control. At other times, announcers would simply read a message handed to them without considering the content first or would not know from whom the message came and therefore whether or not it should be censored. As was true throughout the country, confusion and inconsistency appeared at the radio station. It was particularly significant that some of the Muslim messages got through because the radio was being used as a source of negative propaganda and played a central role in fomenting ethnic polarization. Because they were unable to broadcast their announcements on radio consistently, many Muslim leaders made the same types of announcements in the mosques.

Many Rwandans claimed that their tendency to follow authority was one of the primary drivers of the genocide. This commitment to following leaders, who in the case of Muslims preached positive actions, allowed them to save Tutsis rather than killing them. The leadership's preparation of people against the "temptation" was seen by many Muslims as having inoculated them against the violence that came.

Exceptions

A few members of the Muslim community did join the genocidal killing. Muslims described two members of the government and one leader in the private sector who participated. These people were not viewed, at least in retrospect, as respected members of the community. One had been the head of a newspaper that had incited ethnic polarization. Other Muslims said they had never seen him in a mosque, not even during Ramadan. They said, "He has a Muslim name and a Muslim family, but he did not pray, he did not share anything with the community, so really he was Muslim in name only." With regard to another man who had been a member of government, people in the Muslim community noted that he was "serving other [government] interests" and, thus, no Muslim responded to his appeals for them to participate in the genocide. Non-Muslims also said they did not consider him a Muslim.

In addition, people told a few other stories of Muslims who had behaved badly. Some conspired with the Interahamwe and gave away hiding places, while some even joined the Interahamwe militia. Some of them were said to be willing to kill non-Muslims but not Muslims.

Muslims and many non-Muslims suggested that those Muslims who took part in the killings did so on their own. The Muslim community disassociated itself from those who participated.

Case Writers' Analysis

It is clear that Rwanda's Muslim community behaved in a way that was significantly different from that of the rest of the population.

When the appeal for genocide was launched, Muslims did not feel caught up in that agenda. How was the vast majority of the Muslim community able to respond positively in the face of national madness? Why were Muslims, unlike others across the country, willing to put their identity as Muslims or as human beings above their ethnic identity? People identified several key factors:

1. Lack of direct involvement in the political activities and strife of the country.
2. A lifestyle that reflected solidarity around faith, not Hutu and Tutsi identity.
3. Lived faith on the basis of Islamic principles including nonviolence, nondiscrimination, and helping the oppressed.
4. Memory of the political and social relationships with Tutsis in the past (however, no one felt that, had the situation been reversed such that Tutsis were killing Hutus, Muslims would have joined in).
5. The close physical proximity of living together, which allowed Muslims to defend themselves and to protect others. This also meant that they could more easily communicate with each other when under threat.

Interwoven in these factors were ideas about the role of identity—that is, of how the community understood itself, and of how Muslims understood their own history and used it to justify their nonparticipation. Muslims and non-Muslims cited the community's social cohesion as a key defining characteristic. This was important both in terms of a community identity that erased ethnicity as a relevant defining factor, and in the distinction from the rest of Rwandans that allowed Muslims to feel that "it was not our war."

The fact that Rwandans in general tended to follow their leaders while the Muslim leadership urged nonparticipation in the violence was critical. As well, because Muslim settlements had their own administration separate from the state leadership and political system, the settlements were kept outside of, and felt separate from, political developments in the country. But it may still be asked why the Muslim leadership took this position.

Muslims provided two main reasons. First, their Islamic faith and the teachings of the Quran were always named as fundamental to their position. Second, people cited the Muslim community's separation as a whole from the political system meant that their leaders were not aligned with any political side. Denied access to the political structures, Muslim leaders were not drawn into the same divisive identity politics as the rest of the Rwandan power structure. Muslim religious leaders did not perceive themselves to have a stake in the violence. The historical marginalization in political, physical, social, educational, and economic terms increased social cohesion within the community, including among the leadership, with Muslims seeing themselves as distinct from those who had marginalized them. Because it was not socially easy to be Muslim, this reinforced the spirituality of all who identified themselves as Muslim, because this had broad implications for how one lived.

All of these factors—their Islamic faith, their historical separation from the politics of Rwanda, their physical proximity to each other in settlements and the nature of their leadership—decreased the importance of ethnicity and pushed the Muslim community toward nonparticipation and protection of others rather than violence.

Note

1. Gourevitch, *We Wish to Inform You*, p. 87.

Part 3

Conclusion

13

The Relevance of Nonwar Communities

We should not romanticize the nonwar communities explored in this book. Many of them compromised things they cared about to appease armed groups. People were sometimes killed. Internal dispute resolution systems were necessary because community members had real disagreements. Maintaining solidarity required constant effort in the face of uncertainty. Nonwar communities were made up of real people, with real emotions, trying to live normal lives under extraordinarily difficult circumstances.

Moreover, these nonwar communities had little apparent impact on the broader wars that surrounded them. Although many welcomed all comers, offering them physical support and relative safety, most made no attempt to persuade other communities to follow their lead. With two exceptions (the bishop of Madhu in Sri Lanka and the spirit Mungoi in Mozambique, who was said by his followers to have been active in the Rome negotiations for peace), these communities and their leaders did not enter the politics of conflict resolution and work to end the larger war. Again with two exceptions (the nations of Burkina Faso and Fiji), the conflict prevention strategies of these nonwar communities did not translate into more comprehensive strategies to address the underlying schisms in the societies. And only in Rwanda did the nonwar community actively attempt to prevent and counter the negative impacts of the conflict on others besides themselves. Largely, these communities focused on achieving a strategic goal within their own group. Beyond that, they did not exert, or attempt to exert, influence.

So why are these communities of broader interest? In the introduction to this book, we noted that war is, oddly, an unnatural institution. Statistically, more countries do not engage in war than do, and where war occurs, more people do not actively participate than do. War is in this sense a fragile undertaking; most people want to avoid it.

We also noted that, nonetheless, war continues to be common, enduring, and persistent. It appears that people and societies slip into warfare almost without thought if they feel threatened by others. Although people want to avoid war, most accept that it is "natural" and "necessary" to fight for certain values. But if most people want to avoid war and its costs are so high, why is it also common? If war requires an unnatural effort, why does conflict prevention remain elusive?

The nonwar communities whose experiences are explored in this book are of interest precisely because they did not slip into warfare without thought. They did not think it was natural or necessary. They are of interest because they rejected the "powerlessness" claimed by other communities facing similar circumstances. They set themselves apart not only from their wars, but also from a prevailing human tendency to accept that "forces beyond our control" determine our realities.

They are of interest because they chose a different way and survived—and did so with vigor and self-confidence. They are of interest because their broad experience, taken as a whole, demonstrates the potential of normal people to collectively invent strategies for preventing conflict. Without models or precedents to follow, they originated strategies for exempting themselves from conflicts that overwhelmed others.

Analysis

The other chapters of this book have gathered and explored the many angles of the experiences of these communities and have extracted the lessons and guidance these experiences afford. There is no reason to reiterate or summarize these here. Instead, we take this space to highlight some of our own reflections as we encountered and worked with the evidence of these cases. We were, as we suspect readers of this book will be, impressed and inspired by the stories of these communities. But are there really models here that have relevance for wider conflict prevention, or is each situation unique and thus, though interesting, unmatchable?

Although our strong sense that there is broader relevance is surely clear by now, we acknowledge that there will be no definitive answer to this question unless and until this is proved by others who effectively learn from, adapt, and use the kinds of strategies explored in this book. What we do know is that these communities revealed no single "model" for conflict prevention that can be packaged and exported to other conflicts.

The Underbelly of Ideological Positions

In our own work for development, peace, and social justice, we have ourselves been comfortable with strong expressions of values and have taken positions informed by ideals. We were challenged, therefore, when we observed that these nonwar communities were not ideologically driven. We were surprised that they rested their choices almost entirely (with Rwandan Muslims being the exception) on pragmatic calculations and that they even explicitly eschewed ideology. We felt a bit uneasy that their strategies sometimes entailed what they called "compromises" that could be seen by others as "capitulation" or "selling out."

These communities, however, operated in contexts where armed groups claimed to be driven by ideologies of "ethnic superiority," "national security," or "religious purity." They were all too aware of the violence and hatred spawned by ideological claims.

Our close look at how these communities held to their own values, ensuring that these were not undermined as they engaged with people who held opposing values, prompted us to reexamine how those of us who work internationally describe our motivations. Too often it seems the language of "universal values" becomes associated with political or social ideologies. The weakness, the underbelly, of ideological positioning is that it may prompt intolerance and limit, rather than open, mutual listening and appreciation for difference. We were reminded that attempts to maintain ideological purity in a complex world can, and too often do, either result in irrelevance or, much worse, produce a chain of misunderstanding, intolerance, exclusion, and dominance.

These nonwar communities, who focused on maintaining community-held values through strategies embedded in a hardheaded analyses of their circumstances, reminded us of the value of principaled pragmatism.

The Underbelly of Models

Similar to the dangers of being ideologically driven are the dangers, and weaknesses, of "models." The successes of these nonwar communities demonstrated unequivocally the central importance of accessible, accountable leadership and systems of consultation that give voice to all citizens. These are ideas that are often promoted by those of us who engage internationally. However, discussions of these ideas too often slip into the language of ideals. We initiate programs and projects for "good governance" and "democracy" and "civil society"—concepts that are implicitly, or explicitly, interpreted according to Western models. International efforts encourage the formation of political parties, elections, representative governing bodies, and police and court systems that are based on institutional forms that have worked in Western democracies.

But as noted in previous chapters, these nonwar communities achieved good governance and citizen involvement through an impressive array of forms. Except in the case of Fiji, we simply did not hear stories of civil society groups applying pressure to leadership. The interactions described between the shura council and the people in Jaghori, between Muslims and mullahs in Rwanda, between the mayor and the citizens of Tuzla, between village councils and the people in Manipur and the Philippines, between the spirit Mungoi and the residents in Chidenguele, and between low-profile leaders of the Colombian villages and the people there, were more organic and fluid than oppositional and corrective. People repeatedly expressed their sense that leaders could be held accountable, but even in Afghanistan, where a very unpopular person ran for a seat in the postconflict shura, people reported that they did not confront him but rather that, simply, "he did not receive one single vote."

At the heart of many Western democratic institutions is the notion of majority. We hold campaigns and lobby to convince others of our point of view, and these are followed by elections or votes in which one viewpoint prevails while others fail. In the nonwar communities, people described the processes by which they achieved broad agreement on strategic decisions as consultative and inclusive, and seldom reported them as contentious.

Observing this, we were struck by three things. First was the importance of acknowledging that there are a variety of governance systems through which communities achieve responsible leadership and broad involvement of the people in decisions. One model does not work everywhere. Second, we need to learn to observe more carefully how others disagree with each other and resolve these disagreements. In the West, our systems (especially for those of us who are American) are always vociferous and openly argumentative. Other systems, even though disagreements may be equally profound, are quieter, more conversational than contentious. Just because we don't hear shouting does not mean there is no democracy at work. And third, even as we promote models of good governance, we are inept at the steps that need to be taken to move from an imperfect model to one that is somewhat less flawed, from one that is merely tolerable to one that is better or even excellent. Models seem not to be transferable because they skip interim processes of local adaptation and learning.

The successes of these nonwar communities reminded us that models that work are based in indigenous histories and that, even though they are traditional and familiar, they can then become the bases for new approaches. These communities were not stuck in their old forms but used them to experiment with new, unmodeled strategies to opt out of war.

The Underbelly of Early Warning Systems

Although this thought is not new, the experiences of these nonwar communities caused us to again reflect on the flaws of early warning systems for conflict. We speculate that none of these systems that now exist would have been able to predict that these particular communities would not engage in war. The underbelly of early warning is just that—it is focused on the negative and may therefore put more energy into understanding where and how societal weaknesses may become dangerous than into understanding the forces that exist to counteract these dangers.

Going further, we observe that there is a tendency among international interveners to demonstrate their acumen and sophistication through identifying and interpreting the negative complexity of circumstances. When one points to the potential that a troubled country may not go to war, accusations of naiveté follow. Many of our analytic systems emphasize weaknesses without concomitant care for identifying what is working. In the development and humanitarian assistance fields, we continue to do needs assessments. In conflict prevention work, we identify flash points and divisive leaders.

The successes of these nonwar communities remind us to be attentive, and to learn to be attentive, to existing systems that work. They suggest that if we achieve this, we may find that, with support, already-working systems can be strengthened to have farther-reaching influence on broader political tendencies within countries. If we are right that even in war areas most people do not want to go to war, the potential for this kind of early "alert" system, rather than an early warning system, could be profound.

The fact that these communities survived at all, and did so ultimately with self-confidence, is impressive. Their broad experience, taken as a whole, provides new insights into the potential of normal people to collectively invent strategies for preventing conflict and avoiding violence.

Final Reflection

The world continues to need international mediators and negotiators to confront divisive leaders who take their peoples to war rather than peace. This book does not address this level of conflict prevention or how to do it effectively (other books do). The experiences of these nonwar communities could, however, inform even those efforts, because if international mediators know about and understand the dynamics of localized communities who are exempting themselves from war, they may be able to challenge the claims of divisive leaders about the sources of their conflict and the conditions for resolving it. If nonwar communities exist in virtually all conflict areas, they offer options even to those who must address the politics that divide conflicting parties.

The experiences of these nonwar communities remind us that options exist. They remind us that capacities exist. They teach us that communities of people have the agency to shape things, even in the face of seemingly awful odds, to preserve the values they share and their ways of life. These lessons are not trivial.

Appendix: Project Case Studies

The material in this book is based on the evidence presented in the following thirteen case studies. For those interested in learning more about how the nonwar communities developed their strategies and maintained them, all of these reports are available in full online at www.cdainc.com.

Afghanistan

Suleman, Mohammad, and Sue Williams. "Strategies and Structures in Preventing Conflict and Resisting Pressure: A Study of the Jaghori District, Afghanistan, Under Taliban Control." March 2003.

Bosnia-Herzegovina

Wallace, Marshall, and Vasiliki Neofotistos. "Cross-Ethnic Solidarity in the Face of Ethnic Cleansing." August 2002.

Burkina Faso

Canavera, Mark. "The Spirit of Forgiveness: Tradition, Leadership, and Strategies for Social Cohesion in Burkina Faso." December 2006.

Colombia

Mahony, Liam, and Luis Enrique Eguren. "Territorially Based Alternatives in the Colombian Conflict." July 2004.

Fiji

Doughty, Kristin, Darryn Snell, and Satendra Prasad. "Constraints and Contributors to Violent Conflict in Fiji." May 2003.

India

Butalia, Urvashi. "Interrogating Peace: The Naga-Kuki Conflict in Manipur." September 2005.

Kosovo

Reyes, David. "Community Experiences in Avoiding Conflict." May 2003.

Mozambique

Farmen, Tarah, with Ezequiel Marcos and Egidio Vaz. "Mungoi Community, Chidenguele, Mozambique." August 2005.

Nigeria

Onuoha, Austin, and Lynda Lolo. "Case Study of the Ukwa People of the Niger Delta of Nigeria." May 2004.

Philippines

Iyer, Pushpa. "Peace Zones of Mindanao, Philippines: Civil Society Efforts to End Violence." October 2004.

Rwanda

Doughty, Kristen, and David Moussa Ntambara. "Resistance and Protection: Muslim Community Actions During the Rwandan Genocide." February 2003.

Sierra Leone

Dixon, Lawrence G., and Samuel Mokuwa. "Making Sense of One Community's Experience During War." October 2004.

Sri Lanka

Hansen, Greg. "Madhu Sanctuary in Sri Lanka." June 2003.

Acronyms

ACCU	Self-Defense Militias Córdoba and Urabá
AFP	Armed Forces of the Philippines
ANC	African National Congress
AUC	United Self-Defense Forces of Colombia
BuZa	Ministerie van Buitenlandse Zaken
CDA	Collaborative for Development Action
CIJP	Inter-Congregational Commission for Justice and Peace
EED	Evangelischer Entwicklungsdienst
ELN	Army of National Liberation (Colombia)
EPL	Popular Liberation Army (Colombia)
FARC	Revolutionary Armed Forces of Colombia
Frelimo	Liberation Front of Mozambique
IDP	internally displaced person
LTTE	Liberation Tigers of Tamil Eelam
MILF	Moro Islamic Liberation Front (Philippines)
MNR	Mozambican National Resistance
NATO	North Atlantic Treaty Organization
NGO	nongovernmental organization
Renamo	Mozambican National Resistance
RUF	Revolutionary United Front (Sierra Leone)
SIDA	Swedish International Development Cooperation Agency
SLA	Sierra Leone Army
STEPS	Steps Toward Conflict Prevention
UNHCR	United Nations High Commissioner for Refugees

Bibliography

Anderson, Mary B. *Do No Harm: How Aid Can Support Peace—or War.* Boulder: Lynne Rienner, 1999.

———, ed. *Options for Aid in Conflict: Lessons from Field Experience.* Cambridge, MA: Local Capacities for Peace Project, Collaborative for Development Action, 2000.

Anderson, Mary B., and Peter J. Woodrow. *Rising from the Ashes: Development Strategies in Times of Disaster.* Boulder: Lynne Rienner, 1998.

Bass, Bernard M. *The Bass Handbook of Leadership: Theory, Research, and Managerial Applications.* New York: Free Press, Simon and Schuster, 2008.

The DAC Guidelines on Helping Prevent Violent Conflict. Paris: Organization for Economic Cooperation and Development, Sipa Press, 2001.

Debiel, Tobias, and Martina Fischer. "Crisis Prevention and Conflict Management by the European Union: Concepts, Capacities, and Problems of Coherence." Berghof Report no. 4. Berlin: Berghof Research Center for Constructive Conflict Management, September 2000.

"Early Warning and Early Response: Conceptual and Empirical Dilemmas." Global Partnership for the Prevention of Armed Conflict, Issue Paper no. 1. The Hague: European Centre for Conflict Prevention, September 2006.

Galama, Anneke, and Paul van Tongeren, eds. *Towards Better Peacebuilding Practice: On Lessons Learned, Evaluation Practice, and Aid and Conflict.* Utrecht: European Centre for Conflict Prevention, 2002.

Goodhand, Jonathan, Tony Vaux, and Robert Walker. *Strategic Conflict Assessment.* London: Department for International Development, 2002.

Gormley-Heenan, Cathy. "From Protagonist to Pragmatist: Political Leadership in Societies in Transition." INCORE Research Report. Londonderry: International Conflict Research, University of Ulster and United Nations University, 2001.

Gourevitch, Philip. *We Wish to Inform You That Tomorrow We Will Be Killed with Our Families*. New York: Farrar, Straus, and Giroux, 1998.

Gross Stein, Janice. "Image, Identity, and Conflict Resolution." In Chester A. Crocker and Fen Osler Hampson with Pamela Aall, eds., *Managing Global Chaos: Sources of and Responses to International Conflict*. Washington, DC: US Institute of Peace, 1996.

Lederach, John Paul. *The Moral Imagination: The Art and Soul of Building Peace*. New York: Oxford University Press, 2005.

Lund, Michael. "Conflict Prevention: Policy and Practice in Search of a Theory." In Jacob Berkovitch, Victor Kremenyk, and William Zartman, eds., *Handbook of Conflict Resolution*. Thousand Oaks, CA: Sage, 2009.

Nordstrom, Carolyn. *A Different Kind of War Story*. Philadelphia: University of Pennsylvania Press, 1997.

Nye, Joseph S. *The Powers to Lead*. New York: Oxford University Press, 2008.

Pouligny, Beatrice. "State-Society Relations and Intangible Dimensions of State Resilience and State Building: A Bottom-Up Perspective." Report for the workshop "Transforming Political Structures: Security, Institutions, and Regional Integration Mechanisms." Florence, Italy, April 2009.

van Tongeren, Paul, Malin Brenk, Marte Hellema, and Juliette Verhoeven, eds. *People Building Peace II: Successful Stories of Civil Society*. Boulder: Lynne Rienner, 2005.

Williams, Carol J. "Sarajevo Threat Is Apparently Defused—Yugoslavia: Serb Leader First Says Followers Are Marching on City, Then He Calls on Them to Stay at Home." *Los Angeles Times*, March 4, 1992.

Index

About the Book

How do ordinary people, neither pacifists nor peace activists, come to decide collectively to eschew violent conflict and then develop strategies for maintaining their nonwar stance despite myriad pressures to the contrary?

Mary Anderson and Marshall Wallace analyze the experiences of thirteen nonwar communities that made conscious—and effective—choices not to engage in the fighting that surrounded them. Tracing the steps that these communities took and the strategies that evolved in each setting in response to local circumstances, the authors find lessons with broader relevance for international efforts to prevent violent conflict.

Mary B. Anderson is the author of *Do No Harm: How Aid Can Support Peace—or War* and *Rising from the Ashes: Development Strategies in Times of Disaster*. She retired from her position as executive director of CDA Collaborative Learning Projects in 2009. **Marshall Wallace** is director of the Do No Harm Project at CDA Collaborative Learning Projects and also directed CDA's Steps Toward Conflict Prevention Project.